Sky Stories

From Flying Cars to Flying Fortresses

Dave Unwin

First Published by Pigs Might Fly Publishing
2021

Pigs Might Fly Publishing

www.pigsmightflypublishing.com

ISBN 978-1-5136-8920-3

Contents

Thanks

This book started out not so much as a 'Labour of Love' or even a 'Labour of Lockdown' but more a 'Labour of Lay-down'. Ivan Shaw, the talented designer of the Europa (the most successful British aircraft of the last 30 years) dropped me an email out of the blue saying how much he'd enjoyed 'Flying out of Lockdown' (Chapter 13) and suggesting that perhaps I should collate some of my better pieces into a book. Initially I was ambivalent, thinking it could be construed as perhaps being a bit egotistical, and didn't really give it much thought. Then, after my unfortunate accident in the Sea Fury *Invincible*, I suddenly found myself with a lot of time on my hands, and gave the idea further consideration. One of the downsides to magazines is that they are by nature ephemeral, and I began to think that at the very least a small anthology of my work might make a nice surprise for my mum and dad.

So here it is.

I'd also like to thank all the people who made this book possible, starting with my long-suffering wife Lizzie, for precise sub-editing, my eldest son Will for designing it and my youngest son George for encouraging me when I doubted myself. Thanks must also (in no particular order) go to Peter Holloway, Thom

Richard, John Romain, Sean Sweeney, Dennis Kochan, Jim Harley, Taras Kiceniuk and Taras Kiceniuk Jr, Tim Darrah, Peter Andrews, Jean Munn, 'Dodge' Bailey, Stu Goldspink, Bob Grimstead, Philip Whiteman, Sue Blunt, Shaun Patrick and Eskil Amdal.
Special thanks to Geoff Hill (the 'Abominable Ulsterman'), Alan Munro (AKA 'Salt One') and AFE's Jeremy Pratt for help and encouragement.
Thanks also to Key Publishing's Adrian Cox for letting me use images taken by Duncan Cubitt and the late Steve Fletcher. Thanks for images must also go to Damien Burke, James Cox, Donny Edwards, Darren Harbar, Jim Lawrence, Keith Richards, Rachel Seed and Keith Wilson.

Chapter 1
Why Fly?

Why fly? I was thinking this just the other day while wading through three piles of unpleasant-looking paperwork. One pile contained reminders regarding renewing my medical, BFR and BGA BI rating; another had info on my VP-1's permit renewal and insurance while the third (and largest!) held news which I planned to refer to while writing my monthly column. The news was all rather grim; airfields closing and fuel prices rising, licensing issues, airspace grabs, mandatory electronic conspicuity etc etc ad nauseum. Bored (and slightly depressed) I did the only sensible thing – and went flying.

It was a beautiful evening and my demeanour was improving exponentially as I approached the airstrip. Flying – or even simply the prospect of flying - is a great tonic. For most people 'the sky's the limit' – but if you can fly, it's simply the start. As they say, "a mile of road will take you a mile, a mile of runway can take you anywhere." I am very lucky in that I get to fly a lot. There's a steady stream of aircraft to test for Pilot magazine; I can fly the tugs at two gliding clubs, I own a share in a glider and – best of all – I have my own aircraft that is based on a delightful farm strip only ten minutes from my house. And – as I work mostly from home -I fly several times a week.

Now, I've never been much given to anthropomorphism, but of the hundreds of different aircraft that I've been lucky to fly, four stand out as having real personalities. And, curiously, they're all single seaters. There's a Piper Pawnee known as 'Old Gasper', a 1931 Buhl Bull Pup called 'Mi Amigo', a Schleicher Ka-6E competition number '433' and my VP-1 G-BIFO (known, unsurprisingly, as '*Biffo*'). Many people sneer at simple, unpretentious machines such as Veeps, but it's been my experience that these are the sort of people who don't actually fly very much! Let's compare it to – say - the PC-12, which I flew recently. As much as I'd loved flying the elegant, sophisticated turboprop, it isn't really the kind of machine that you pull out of the shed by yourself on a warm summer's evening, and then simply pop upstairs for a half-hour bimble at 505ft. Well, *Biffo* is.

Biffo's engine started first swing – now for the challenge of enticing this under-powered machine into the air! I could feel my mood lightening as we raced down the runway, while my spirits rose along with the needle of the altimeter. It was good to be back in the sky. The slipstream was racing past the open cockpit like an icy waterfall and the engine was revving right up to the red line. It's a heady, intoxicating combination and my senses (with perhaps the exception of my hearing!) were alive to any possibility. Now, where to go? With just a gentle pressure on the stick and rudder pedals I could make the whole world appear to revolve around me – how cool is that? I decided to follow the shoreline of Rutland Water. With my left elbow resting comfortably on the leather cockpit sill and a full, unobstructed 360° view above the wings it's a wonderful way to clear the mind. It was Saint-Exupery who wrote, "I fly because it releases my mind from the tyranny of petty things" – a sentiment I completely agree with.

The light had taken on the wonderfully sublime quality that you often get in the hour before sunset and the wings glowed in the soft, suffused sunlight. For the thousandth time, I appreciated just how pretty England's patchwork fields are. I spotted a balloon towards the south and considered chasing it, but a scrap of cumulus had appeared above the disused airfield of North Luffenham and I decided to investigate that instead. With only 60 horses available I take every opportunity to increase *Biffo's* total energy by using the atmosphere for fuel and my limited intellect as an auxiliary engine. Like most other wood-and-fabric flying machines, *Biffo* is an aircraft that flies upon the air, not through it. Consequently, any rising air can and should always be exploited. I spiralled swiftly up to 3,000ft on what must have been the last thermal of the day, and then headed for home while trading height for speed.

From the end of the downwind leg I flew a single graceful sweeping curve, then rolled the wings level on short final. The throttle only ever moved backwards – to add power is an admission of misjudgement. A gentle flare, a brief floating moment then all three wheels simultaneously brushed the grass. In my opinion, the subtle and sublime shifting of weight from wing to wheel is profoundly gratifying when it all comes together - and doubly so on a grass runway.

I taxied back in with a big grin, basking in the smug satisfaction of knowing that not only could I not have done it any better, but anyone watching couldn't have done it any better either. I snapped the switches off, and having had the raucous *blat blat blat* of an unsilenced Volkswagen engine assaulting my ears for the previous hour the sudden silence was profound. I slipped my leather helmet off, and as my hearing began to return to normal the sounds of evening slowly unfolded, along with the whirling diminuendo of the single gyro as it slowly spun to a stop. Before climbing out I studied the sky, watching the last few scraps of cumulus dissolve into nothingness and wondered if it'll be flyable tomorrow. It's a good time to think; sometimes I'll even jot down a few notes – just as I'm doing now.

Ultimately, that flight had not only helped me write this piece but also answered my initial question. All pilots know that the sky is always waiting, but never impatient.

So, why fly?

Because I can.

Chapter 2
Supermarine Spitfire Tr.9

As the Spitfire sliced skyward with the roar of the mighty Merlin thundering in my ears I couldn't help sneaking a glance at the evocative elliptical wing. I'm back in the cockpit of a Spitfire – but this time I'm sitting in the front! Can it get any better? I've waited two years for this moment, but as I merely think about turning and the Spitfire responds to my every whim, I know it's been worth the wait!

Interestingly, the Spitfire is probably the most developed fighter ever made. The Mk. I, which entered service in 1938, had a 990hp engine and a MAUW of 2,595kg. Ten years later, the

Mk.24 had 2,035hp, and weighed up to 5,511kg! It was also the only fighter that was in production before the Second World War started, and remained in production after it had ended.

Access to the cockpit is quite good - the canopy slides back a fair way, there is a small door on the left side and the non-slip wingroot walkway is sensibly sized.

Having slid the canopy back and slipped into the cockpit, I made myself comfortable. An unusual facet of the Spitfire's cockpit (and I suspect many other RAF fighters of the 1940s) is that there is no floor. Consequently, it is very important not to drop anything. The seat and rudder pedals adjust over a good range, so once I was satisfied that I could reach everything and that the view over the nose was as good as it was going to get, I began to study the cockpit more closely. It is typically British, a mixed-up medley of mostly black-faced dials in a black-painted panel, along with some guarded buttons and a few warning lights seemingly scattered at random. Indeed, there are some aspects (such as having the undercarriage selector on the right, or installing the rudder trim wheel in the vertical plane) that, if this were a prototype, I would deem distinctly unsatisfactory!

The tall control column features the classic British spade grip, which incorporates a single lever for the wheel brakes and a large button

for the cannons and machine-guns. Two particularly peculiar aspects of the primary controls are that the control column articulates just below the spade grip and that the rudder pedals slide fore-and-aft. They can be adjusted via the star wheels built into the tubes that the pedals are mounted on.
John Romain climbed quickly into the rear cockpit and I ran through the checks. As the coolant heats up very quickly, checks like the 'full and free' for the controls and setting the trims are done long before starting the engine. Starting the Spitfire can be compared to being a 'one-armed paper-hanger' as quite a few controls must be operated more-or-less simultaneously, but the big Merlin was soon snarling, the prop a silver blur and I was ready to roll.
The Spitfire was practically shaking with suppressed energy, and it almost felt as if I was riding an impossibly powerful horse. As we set off on the long taxi to Duxford's runway 06 I noticed an old man standing at the fence and staring with rapt interest at the Spitfire. What was he looking at, I wondered? A piece of history – or a piece of his story? I continued along the taxiway in a series of sinuous S-turns, while carefully monitoring the coolant temperature and brake triple pressure gauges. Taxiing a Spitfire is not easy. The big nose blocks out a considerable amount of whatever's immediately in front, and this –

combined with a castoring tailwheel and hand-operated pneumatic brakes – make it quite a challenging exercise. Obviously, for several reasons you can't go too fast, but at the same time you can't go too slow, because the coolant temperature is constantly rising. Luckily for me it was a cool day. It must be a nightmare when it's hot, particularly if you've got a long taxi.

At the run-up point I swung the aircraft into wind, centred the rudder pedals and squeezed the brake lever. During the briefing John had emphasised that you never set the parking brake for the run up, as should the tail start to lift (and it will at the slightest opportunity) you must allow the aircraft to roll forward. As the oil temperature was already over 40°C I ensured the stick was fully back and slowly opened the throttle to 1,850rpm to check the mags and exercise the prop, then slowly pulled the throttle right back to idle and noted the rpm. This is very important. The Spitfire is not over-endowed in the flap department, and if the tick-over is too high it will float a considerable distance.

John then showed me a very useful trick. He directed me to roll slowly forwards about half the aircraft's length, then turn 45°. By looking back over my shoulder I could see if any oil or coolant had leaked onto the ground during the run-up.

All checks complete, I trundled out onto the grass runway, lined up and took a deep breath. I'd already noted that the wind was from the left, which would tend to exacerbate the Spitfire's propensity to swing. Brakes off, I slowly opened the throttle while feeding in right rudder. I'm so paranoid about not letting the Spitfire swing that I focussed all my attention outside. Consequently, I used more power than I meant to (+12lb/sq in boost, instead of only +7) and we were off the ground very quickly.

I felt the throttle move back under my hand as John accurately set the power while commenting dryly "plus seven is plenty, Dave!" I'm annoyed I've used too much power, but pleased that I haven't swung. As the last of the runway disappears from view I squeezed the brakes, put my left hand on the stick and my right on the undercarriage lever. There's a slight wobble as I changed hands, but it's not too bad. I pressed down on the lever for four seconds (to pressurise the hydraulic system), moved it inwards (out of its gate) and forwards in one movement, then held it in place while waiting for the red 'wheels up' light.

It is imperative that the undercarriage retracts completely, as the legs are immediately in front of the radiators. Without an adequate flow of air through the radiators and oil cooler the engine will rapidly overheat. I could feel the wheels thump home in the wells through my seat, and this was confirmed by the red light. Changing hands again, I rolled in some nose down trim and pulled the power back to +2 and 2,000rpm. Phew! So far – so good!

I then eased the prop back to 1,850rpm, left the boost at +2 and took a couple of moments to savour where I was sitting – the front seat of a Spitfire! I gazed out over the impossibly long nose and then looked sideways at the evocative elliptical wing. Just for a couple of minutes, I completely forgot about John sitting just behind me and revelled in the Spitfire's grace, elegance and power. Then, it was time to get back to work.

After a couple of graceful, sweeping turns I tried to work out where we were. However, it was a rather grey, claggy day – and at 220mph we'd already gone a long way. Consequently, I was 'temporarily unsure of our position'. John helpfully gave me a heading to steer, and told me to slow down prior to extending the undercarriage and flaps.

Despite pulling the power back to -2 the Spitfire was reluctant to decelerate, so I initiated a gentle climb to shed some speed. I've memorised the limiting speeds, and as the needle of the ASI dipped below 160mph I changed hands, pressed the undercarriage lever forwards (to get the legs off the uplocks) and pulled it all the way back in one movement. As the legs locked down I added some nose-up trim, waited for the speed to reduce below 120mph, then lowered the flaps. I felt the deceleration as they extended into the airstream, and the nose also pitched down, requiring more nose up trim.

At 105mph I eased the *Spit* into a smooth right turn to remind myself how it would feel on the approach. It felt like the lateral control was beginning to degrade slightly as the speed reduced, although there was still lots of lift in those beautiful wings. However, the elevator remained very effective. Satisfied that I'd got the feel of it, John directed me to increase rpm to 2,000 and the boost to +2, retract the flaps and undercarriage, and return to Duxford.

I entered the circuit at Duxford via a 'run and break'. However, this wasn't for show. As I'd already learnt, because the aircraft is a relatively 'clean' design it takes time to slow it down. The best way to bleed energy is to pull up and round, putting on some 'g' in the process.

I was careful to avoid Duxford village via a small dogleg as I turned downwind, then moved quickly into position so that I was at 800ft agl with the wingtip just level with the runway. I made a quick check of the speed midfield, then lowered the undercarriage, retrimmed and opened the oil cooler and radiator doors. After another speed check, it was time for 'flaps down', more nose-up trim and then bank back towards the runway. The flaps are pneumatic, as are the brakes, so I

glanced at the brake triple pressure gauge and checked we had adequate pressure.
As I came around the corner I thought "I'm a bit low" and asked if I should add power. "No, it's OK – keep it coming," John replied. I pushed the prop up and slowly started rolling the wings level on very short final. "Nice," said John, "OK, power off!"
I slowly closed the throttle and ever so gently eased the stick back. The nose reared up, blocking my view forwards. Using my peripheral vision, I tried to hold the attitude I'd burned into my memory – I didn't want to touch down tail first. For long seconds the Spitfire floated tantalisingly close to the ground, and then settled gently onto the grass. We were down and rolling out nice and straight. I could feel that the elevator was still very effective, and slowly eased it back as the speed dropped. On many taildraggers, you want to get the stick right back straightaway, but the Spit has big wings and a powerful elevator. I could sense that it still wanted to fly.
As briefed, I ignored the brakes and just used small jabs of rudder to keep us straight. The grass would slow us down. As the speed dropped away I tried a couple of very tentative squeezes of brake, and we slowed to a stop. I suddenly remembered to start breathing again, and raised the flaps. It was a good landing, and I know it!

A fair chunk of tailwheel time, some excellent coaching and a bit of luck had produced a smooth three-pointer! “Very nice,” said John. I was well chuffed. As I taxied carefully back on the grass he added, “this time, I want to see the power come in smoothly. Let’s see a nice steady 1, 2, 3, 4, 5, 6, 7 on the boost gauge – not a jerky 1…3…5…8…12!”

We both laughed, but I resolved to ‘do it right’ next time– and I did. The take-off was much better this time. The power was applied smoothly to +7lbs sq in boost, and I barely wobbled when I changed hands to raise the undercarriage. Speeds, heights and power settings were all good as I turned back downwind. I really felt as if I was ‘in the groove’, and John was saying nothing.

“Here we go,” I thought to myself. “This looks perfect! OK – gear down, open the oil cooler and radiator doors, trim. Flaps down, more trim – check the air pressure, round we go. I’m just ever so slightly slow,” I thought, “so just a tad more power…there. The angle looks good, the speed is dropping back towards 90mph, start rolling the wings level and push the…” “Prop please Dave,” says John. Bugger! He beat me to it. If only I’d been talking out loud! I slowly drew off the power and felt the throttle move ever so slightly under my hand as John ensured that it was on the stop. Even a small amount of residual thrust would greatly prolong the float.

I was holding off and trying to keep it airborne - then the wheels touched, but we still had flying speed. We then hit a bump which skipped us back into air, and suddenly we were flying again.

During the briefing John had said that this was a distinct possibility, and that under no circumstances should I try and 'chase' the attitude, as a PIO (Pilot Induced Oscillation) is almost inevitable due to the sensitive elevator. Instead, I held the stick still, kept straight with rudder and waited. Two more small skips and we were down and rolling out. I'd done it!

Back at the hangar I pulled out the idle/cut-off ring and the great propeller swiftly slowed to a stop. Even before I'd got the switches off John had unstrapped and was climbing out, but I was in no rush. Instead, I sat in the cockpit and tried to remember everything. The feel of the spade grip in my hand, the awesome cowling stretching out in front of me and the heady aroma of oil, Avgas and a hot V-12. Reluctantly I undid my harness and took one last look around the cockpit. What an incredible experience!

Chapter 3
Just Up

It'd been grim. A nasty bout of Manflu and unseasonably poxy weather had kept me ground-bound for a whole week, and the low cloud and drizzly rain have mirrored my mood. On the seventh day I finally felt airworthy, but the weather wasn't co-operating. A clearance was forecast, but it was late. Finally, at 1800hrs, it was if a curtain had been lifted across the stage of the sky. Official sunset was at 1933, so I hurried to the airfield, arriving just in time to see a giant rainbow drifting away downwind – it looked absolutely amazing, and I took it as a good omen. I'm very lucky in that not only is *Biffo* based close to my house, but he is always at the front of hangar. Consequently, within twenty minutes of leaving home *Biffo* is standing outside, bathed in beautiful evening sunlight. As we usually fly together at least twice a week he looked at me almost accusingly, as if to say, "where've you been?" So far, I'd been rushing, but as I slipped the chocks in front of the wheels I deliberately slowed things down. Having checked the fuel and oil, it was a careful pre-flight and then the time-honoured ritual of pumping the primer, setting the choke, sucking in and then selecting the mags on. "C'mon *Biffo*" I muttered to myself, "wakey wakey". A deft flip of the toothpick prop and the little engine barked joyously into life and settled down to a smooth, easy growl. The friendly farmer heard *Biffo* start, so he wandered up from the farm to say 'hi' and generously offered to hoist the windsock while I get my kit on. By the time I'd donned scarf, jacket, helmet and gloves the oil was warm and *Biffo* is rocking slightly on his wheels; it almost looks as if he is fidgeting impatiently, eager to get back in the air. Within minutes we were racing down the strip and up into the sky.

As we climbed slowly towards the west-north-west the sun sank majestically below the horizon. The fantastical cloud shapes and wonderful colours reminded me of a Turner painting. I swung *Biffo* through a great sweeping arc across the velvet sky, and noticed that the full moon has slipped out from behind a cloud. It looked incredible and I thought – as I often do – is it really almost 40 years since someone last stood on its surface? As we continued to spiral skyward I was entranced and delighted by just how beautiful the sky had become. A stunning sunset and marvellous moonrise –what a flight! The air was warm and smooth, *Biffo* was running like a noisy sewing machine and everywhere I looked was wonderful. It's just so true – there's no place like cloudbase. Thus far, I had directed all my attention upwards, but as I drifted over the A1 I realised with a start that every car had its lights on. This mundane road had become impossibly glamorous – it looked like a river of diamonds. However, when I glanced back towards where I know the strip is I became acutely aware that darkness was stealing stealthily across the ground at a thousand miles an hour, and swallowing everything in its path. *Biffo's* only electrical systems are his twin magnetos – we have no lights (not even a torch) and it's definitely getting dark. Time to go home. I rolled *Biffo* up onto his port wingtip and then let the nose drop. As we slid down through the warm sky towards the welcoming earth I saw a flash of white wings in the gathering gloom. A barn owl (named - rather appositely - Barney by my two sons) has taken up residence in the old barn behind my house, and I wondered fleetingly if perhaps he also couldn't resist the joy of flight on such a beautiful evening. More practically but less prosaically, he probably wanted to catch his evening meal. *Biffo's* wheels kissed the ground at 2002, and by the time he was safely ensconced back in his hangar it was truly dark. As I wandered across the strip to lower the windsock the Lincolnshire countryside was busy with the ways of night. The windsock was starkly silhouetted against the evening sky, and as I reached it an owl hooted mockingly somewhere in the night. I wondered if it's Barney laughing at me because he can fly in the dark and *Biffo* can't.

Back home, seven-year-old Will has just gone to bed, so I go up to tuck him in. "Good flight, Dad?" he asks. "Yeah, great thanks Will" I reply, tousling his hair fondly. He wants more detail (anything to delay going to sleep!), so I tell him about the rainbow, the sunset, the moonrise and all the other wonderful sights. He is impressed, although he clearly struggles with the concept of the A1 looking glamorous!

"And where did you go? he asks.

"Nowhere in particular" I shrug, "just up."

Chapter 4
Taylor Aerocar 1

For almost as long as there have been cars and aircraft, designers have dreamed of merging the two technologies. In fact (and not only incredibly but also somewhat unlikely) the very first attempt at building a flying car can be traced as far back as 1912! However, the three most significant attempts to produce an airworthy automobile are the 1937 Aerobile, the Airphibian of 1947 and easily the most successful, the Taylor Aerocar.
The 1957 issue of 'Jane's All The World's Aircraft' described the Aerocar as "a convertible aeroplane and road vehicle which incorporates a number of features not

introduced in craft of this type". It would have been more accurate if it had said, "incorporates a number of features not introduced in craft of *any* type". For example, the prototype had front-wheel drive, wishbone suspension units on all four axles and used a significant amount of fibreglass in its construction – in 1949! However, and even more impressively, quite apart from the sheer audacity of designing and building a flying car, Taylor successfully achieved something that is even harder – certification!

November 102D is an Aerocar I, and was the fourth one built. Owned by Ed Sweeney and regularly flown by his son Sean, it is easily the most active of all the Aerocars made. It essentially comprises two separate units – a four-wheel, two-seat car, and a quickly detachable flight module which consists of the wings, empennage, tail and propeller. Designing a flying car poses many problems. For example, whenever we talk about the weight of an aeroplane, we must also and always consider the balance. The location of the CG of a car, and that of an aeroplane, are far from compatible. The aircraft's CG needs to be just in front of the rear wheels (so that it can rotate to take off and land), while the car's needs to be much further forward (otherwise the front wheels will not have adequate grip). Talking of wheels, the undercarriage presented myriad engineering challenges. An aircraft's undercarriage is not designed to corner, or indeed sustain any appreciable side loads. Similarly, a car is not intended to absorb vertical speeds of up to 600ft/min. The engine - a Lycoming O-360 air-cooled flat-four, de-rated to 148hp - is mounted facing backwards, and is located below and behind the seats, just forward of the rear wheels.

Upon settling into the left seat, I began to study the controls and instruments very carefully. At first glance, it does look more like the cabin of a car than the cockpit of an aircraft. The control yoke resembles a steering wheel (although the top is flat) and has a horn button in the centre, as any 1950s' airworthy automobile should. It is linked to the front wheels for control on the ground, and to the ailerons and elevators for control in the air. The gauges (apart from the flight instruments obviously) look a lot more automotive than aeronautical.

A centre-mounted Vernier throttle controls the engine, while a large T-handle above the throttle adjusts the trim. So far, so good – but looking down at my feet I could see no fewer than five pedals, plus a small foot switch to dip the headlights! From left to right, these are the left rudder pedal, clutch, brake, accelerator and right rudder pedal. A small, floor-mounted lever selects the gears in the three-speed box.

With the practically un-silenced engine blaring boisterously just behind my ears, I'd never been more grateful for a pair of noise-cancelling headphones as I trundled along the taxiway. The first lesson I had to learn was that on the ground the Aerocar is steered by the control wheel, not the rudder pedals. Sean suggested that I place both my feet on the floor while taxiing, and this certainly helped. The pre-take-off checks are very simple, and having carefully lined up with the centreline I consciously placed my feet back on the rudder pedals, took a deep breath and smoothly opened the throttle.

The acceleration – although not startling – was perfectly adequate, and I had no difficulty keeping straight. I held just a little bit of forward pressure on the control wheel to ensure that the front wheels had plenty of grip. Again, this is counter-intuitive to usual procedure – but the Aerocar is far from 'usual'! At 55mph I rotated and the Aerocar climbed away quite convincingly. I would guess we used about 350m of runway, and our initial climb rate was about 500ft/min. Although by modern standards these numbers are nothing special, for a 1950s' two-seater they are perfectly acceptable. As I turned downwind (having checked behind me with the rear-view mirror!) I began to get a real feel for the Aerocar.

While flying from the right seat I'd already got the impression that the controls were quite mushy, and it sort of felt as if all the cables were slightly stretched. However, on the plus side the visibility was much better than I'd expected. (I don't know why I had any expectations, having never flown a flying car before, but there you are!)
As I proceeded from base on to final I noted that although it didn't seem to be particularly well damped in roll, it was quite stable in pitch. I used 80mph on final, and after a brief float was rewarded with a smooth touchdown on the rear wheels. Having gently lowered the front wheels on to the ground (to maintain directional control) I opened the throttle wide and took off for another circuit. This time I went slightly further downwind for a longer, flatter final approach. This worked well (due to the poor aileron authority you really don't want any appreciable amount of bank anywhere near the ground). The landing was good, and the take-off even better! I must admit that I had approached testing this flying car with a small amount of trepidation. After all, I knew that it would obviously have certain idiosyncrasies, and would definitely be outside my normal frames of reference. However, my fears proved to be unfounded. I can fly this car!
As we headed back towards Kissimmee I used some of the powerful Florida thermals to boost

our climb rate because I wanted to examine the stall characteristics and thought that another couple of thousand feet might prove prudent. When I'd asked Sean about the stall characteristics, he replied that he didn't know, as neither he nor his dad had ever stalled it. However, it is a fully certificated aeroplane, and the forward CG (I was constantly carrying a lot of nose-up trim) convinced me that the stall wouldn't be especially dramatic. In fact, it took a lot of effort to stall it at all.

That thick wing is obviously a slow-speed section, and even when I got the nose well above the horizon with the control wheel on the backstop, it 'mushed' more than stalled, and simply descended straight ahead with a high sink rate and the nose gently hunting in pitch. I never actually heard the stall warning horn (which doubles as the car horn) but could feel just a small amount of buffet through the stick at about 45mph.

An examination of the stick-free stability revealed the Aerocar to be strongly positive longitudinally, positive directionally and weakly positive laterally. However, the combination of slightly miss-rigged ailerons and quite strong thermals made the lateral stability difficult to evaluate accurately.

With the power set at 25/25 we cruised steadily back towards Kissimmee at 105mph indicated, while I slowly mastered the gentle lateral PIO that seemed to be a feature of

Aerocar flying. I eventually learnt that the trick is to not chase the roll excursions but simply make small control inputs with the ailerons and wait. It certainly isn't crisp (in fact, at times the lateral control does feel quite soggy) but if you're patient and don't make big corrections, it will settle down. Incidentally, the still-air range as either a car or an aeroplane is exactly the same – 400 miles.

Back at Kissimmee there was a bit of a crosswind, but it was nothing to a veteran flying-car pilot like me (hey, with over two hours on type I'm one of the most experienced – and current – Aerocar pilots in the world!) and I greased it on.

As I taxied onto the apron outside Warbird Adventures, Sean directed me to angle the nose away from the hangar, and then stop. "You've got to have the full Aerocar experience," he grinned, "so clutch in, select reverse gear and back us up!" I did as I was told, while taking care to not even look at the wheel brake. If you do brake while reversing it sits on its tail. While not dangerous (there is a skid at the base of the fin) it certainly doesn't look good. Thus far, I was very pleased with myself, and was anxious not to screw up at this stage of the game. I could see that this could be a very useful feature. Imagine you're on a narrow taxiway and need to make a 180. For many aircraft this could be tricky, but all

you do in an Aerocar is pop it in gear and make a three-point turn!
So, I was more than happy that it is a perfectly viable aircraft, but what would it be like as a road vehicle? (Incidentally, no Aerocar has ever been damaged in flight, only on the road).
Obviously, the first thing to do was de-rig it, and this once again gave me the opportunity to appreciate the elegant engineering. Firstly, a small drag pin is pulled, allowing that wing to be rotated through 90° and then carried back and hung on the tail. As the wing is pivoted back its aileron simultaneously and automatically folds up to facilitate this. Once both wings are hanging from the tail, the leading edges of the wing roots are opened and small wheels cranked out. The wing struts are removed and clipped in place, the electrics disconnected and surprisingly quickly the flight module was disengaged from the car. This was then turned through 180° and attached to the back of the vehicle, the electrics were reconnected and it was ready for towing.
I particularly liked the brake lights (which are built into the wingroots) and the zip-up cover with protects the flight module's prop shaft. However, my favourite feature is that to connect that flight module's drive shaft to the 'Flexidyne', you flip up the number plate. Honestly, it's like something out of a James Bond film!

I then took the Aerocar for a quick drive around the airfield. As you'd imagine, it's quite a sprightly performer, even though the accelerator is deliberately restricted to only give about one third of the available power.

"Well, Dave' asked Sean as I pulled up next to the hangar and shut the engine down, "what do you think?" "I reckon that compared to a Cessna, it's a fine car," I replied, "while on balance with a Buick, it's a hell of an aeroplane." "Exactly!" he grinned. "Now all we have to do is make it amphibious."

Chapter 5
Clouds

It hadn't been much good for flying but then I realised that a cold front was forecast to go through around midnight, bringing with it some much dryer, fresher air. That evening I laid out my flying kit, checked the NOTAMs and set my alarm clock.

The next morning the front garden shimmered and shone beneath a heavy frost. I now clearly understand the phrase "blade of grass" as it seemed that a million tiny steel swords had been planted in the ground by an army of miniature warriors. The vast vault of the sky is ice blue, but the glowing yellow orb of the morning sun is compelling. Breakfast and coffee consumed, it's time to dress. I've often said that one should always dress appropriately for the occasion, and on this occasion it's going to be cold! Layer after layer goes on, and then it's off to the strip. *Buzz* seems to share my enthusiasm for the day, and starts instantly. While the little VW engine warms up I put a few more layers on, and then wedge myself into the tiny cockpit. Minutes later and the raucous cacophony of a barely-silenced Beetle motor at full chat shatters the stillness as *Buzz* races across the frozen turf. There's almost no wind but the cold, crisp air is thick with lift, and after barely a hundred metres I sense the wing taking the weight and just *think* about flying. There's that magical, almost mystical metamorphosis as my curious contraption of metal, wood and fabric somehow changes into a lithe, gravity defying flying machine, the wheels stop their urgent pattering and *Buzz* slides into the sky. All right! It never grows old, and I hope it never will. I love flying early in the morning; - the air seems to sparkle – fresh, pure and full of possibilities. We arrow upward in a long, graceful slant and as the horizon slowly begins to expand the opening lines of one of my favourite poems, 'Per Ardua', suddenly springs to mind. "They that have climbed the white mists of the morning, they that have soared before the world's awake."

After pleasantly bimbling about low-level for an hour or so I notice that a few, wispy cumulus are beginning to form and decide to climb above them. Approaching the diaphanous flanks of the cloud it becomes apparent that the tops of the quickly-forming cumulus are rising faster than *Buzz* is, so I circle around to the sunward-side and enjoy the spectacle of my trusty little aeroplane's shadow against the dazzlingly snow-white cloud. Interestingly, the cloud is continuing to grow, becoming bigger and more solid with every second. A large, canyon-like crack has appeared on one side and I plunge joyously though it. From a distance this cloud now probably looks quite substantial, but up close its ethereal nature is obvious, and *Buzz* plunges through the gap with wisps of white vapour swirling around his wingtips. Bursting out onto the other side I convert my speed into height and swing back towards the translucent top. The cloud has finally stopped growing, and within minutes I'm level with its bulging summit and then climbing above. Despite the cold a grin as wide as the wingspan splits my face; - what a view! There appears to be a quite pronounced inversion, but all over the sky great white icebergs of cloud are bursting through, and it looks absolutely amazing. A practically-full moon completes a truly remarkable sky as I turn to keep the sun on my face, hunker down into the cramped cockpit and look around. Sailing along the sunward edge of the pristine snow white cloud-slopes, I'm struck once again by the beauty of its perfection. It's simply breath-taking, so for several minutes I skim along the sides, frolicking around it like a dolphin playing in a ship's bow wave. At one point I spot *Buzz's* shadow, surrounded by the vivid rainbow hues of one of the most glorious 'glories' I've ever seen. Time seems to compress and expand simultaneously, and the raucous *blat blat blat* of the four little exhausts have faded so that I barely notice them, nor the avalanche of freezing air that is battering against the tiny windscreen. There's something a little special about being above the clouds in an open cockpit, an intoxicating combination of power and poetry that is hard to describe and difficult to resist.

Floating across the vapour floes at a heady 5,000ft I realise that there's less and less ground in view and that perhaps I'd better start down. A gorge appears in a nearby cumulus, and I plunge gratefully through its wispy, misty veils into a dark, shadow world of drab greens and browns. Without the sun everything seems colder now, and I note with considerable pleasure that I'm very close to the strip. My thirst for flight slaked, *Buzz* slides earthward towards the welcoming runway, and settles softly onto the freshly-thawed greensward.

Farmer John approaches with an amused grin on his face as I climb stiffly out of the cockpit. “Cold enough for you was it” he asks, “I didn’t think you’d fly today.” “Well mate” I smilingly reply, “to paraphrase both Oscar Wilde and The Pretenders, - we are all in the gutter, but some of us are looking at the clouds!”

Chapter 6
Boeing B-17G Flying Fortress

"A Fort lives in the sky, from three to six miles up, and the only real things up there are the throttles and the feathering buttons, the engine gauges and the rudder pedals, an oxygen mask full of drool, and a relief can half-full of relief." B-17 co-pilot Lt. Bert Stiles wrote those words seventy years ago in his seminal book 'Serenade to the Big Bird' – and as our Fortress rumbled sedately over Florida I couldn't help but wonder what he'd have thought of our flight. One thing's for sure – the

skies above Winter Haven are a lot more peaceful than Wilhelmshaven's.
'Serenade' is - in my opinion - one of the best-written books to have come out of World War Two, while the Flying Fortress has to be one of the most legendary aircraft of all time. Consequently, when the opportunity arose to fly as a B-17 co-pilot I only had to think about it for no more than a millisecond, and caught up with the Collings Foundation's B-17, B-24 and P-51C at Winter Haven in Florida. The proud old warbirds looked magnificent in the warm winter sun, and I was practically salivating at the prospect of getting behind the controls. Before I was even allowed to sit in it though, the Foundation's Jim Harley started my training the day before, and after an exhaustive ground school session on the Fort's systems, services, speeds, and idiosyncrasies (which took several hours), Jim and I walked out to the brooding bomber.
As we walk slowly around it Jim points out some of its notable features, while I can't help but compare it with the B-24 parked nearby. I soon realise that – unlike the Liberator, there's a lot more oil on the wings, cowlings and ground. "Yup" nods Jim ruefully "those Wright Cyclones sure throw out a lot more oil than a Twin Wasp." Each engine has its own independent fuel system, with a combined capacity of 6,435 litres. To put this into

perspective, a Cessna 172 carries 212 litres of fuel!
As we walk round I notice all the Browning M2 fifty calibre machine-gun barrels protruding from the tail, ball, mid-upper, waist, chin and cheek gun positions. Even though early B-17s weren't as well armed as the G-model, it's not hard to see why Seattle Times reporter Richard Williams exclaimed "why – it's a flying fortress" the first time he saw one. Unfortunately, the machine-gun is not much use against flak, and a particularly sobering statistic is that more than 50% of all the G models built were lost in combat.
Jim emphasises that the Fort is a two-crew aeroplane and that I must play my part as the co-pilot properly, as there are some controls that the captain just can't reach. I'll be flying with Mac McCauley, who's hugely experienced in B-17s (over 5,000 hours) and 'Nine-oh-Nine' is very much his baby. Now, nobody likes to see their baby mistreated and I soon get the impression that Mac can be quite irascible if things aren't done to his satisfaction. Indeed, as Jim continues to explain my duties a lot of the briefing contains the phrases "Mac doesn't like that, "Mac won't like that, and "Mac really doesn't like that". I begin to wonder what I've let myself in for and - that night - spend several hours carefully poring over the checklist.....

I meet Mac the following morning, and – contrary to my expectations - he appears to be in a perfectly affable mood. As we walk out I remember Bert Stiles' description of the Fort. He wrote that "the Boeing B-17 is a good airplane, whether it's made by Boeing or Douglas or Vega. It's a pretty airplane too, in the air. With its wheels down, sitting on the ground, it is a lazy-looking job, with none of the eager look of an A-20 or a B-26. But once a Fort is airborne and the wheels are up, there isn't a prettier airplane in the sky." I wouldn't say that it's exactly pretty, but it certainly has plenty of 'ramp presence' and I'm thrilled – and also honoured – to be its co-pilot.

Once we're securely strapped in, Mac tells me to fish out the checklist from the pocket underneath my side window. Using the 'challenge and response' format we carefully work our way through the list, until we're ready to start. And just as it would've been in 1944, my role today is definitely that of the co-pilot, it being tacitly understood that although I'm welcome to lightly follow through on the controls during take-off and landing and fly the Fortress in the cruise, whenever the wheels are out of the wells Mac will fly. This is how it was in service and furthermore 'Nine-oh-Nine' is one of only 12 airworthy Fortresses, and Mac's baby.

To be honest, I think that even if I had 500 hours in the BBMF Lancaster, Mac would still do the take-off and landing on our first flight together. Having checked that the prop arc of engine number 3 is clear (this one is always started first as it also powers the hydraulic pump) and that our crew chief was standing by with an extinguisher, I seek out the toggle switches for the fuel boost and pre-oil pumps, starters, primers and ignition boost systems. As all the toggle switches look identical and the 'Start' and 'Ignbst' ones operate two engines each, it is vital that I get it right. If – for example – I pre-oil number 1, crank 3, prime 2 and select 'Ignbst' for 4 I'm fairly sure that Mac's sunny disposition will not prevail! But Jim has trained me well, and in no time at all we have the wonderfully liquid rumble of four big round engines filling the cockpit. I continue my way through the checklist and we're soon ready to roll.

"OK Dave" grunts Mac - "let's go. Chocks clear?" "Clear my side" I reply. "Tailwheel unlock, parking brake off" are the next commands – and mis-managing either will incur Mac's displeasure. The tailwheel lock is operated by a lever set in the floor by the co-pilot's seat; it allows the tailwheel to either fully castor or be locked in trail. The locking pin is designed to fail in shear, so it imperative that it is unlocked when turning. The lock/unlock lever must not be forced, while if the park brake knob is not released carefully its return spring is powerful enough to punch a hole in the sub-panel. Mac eases the Fort out of its parking space, and as soon as we're on the taxiway asks for the tailwheel to be locked.

I'm already very impressed by how easily Mac handles this big taildragger. Every time we turn a corner on the way to the runway its "unlock tailwheel" – "tailwheel unlocked" followed by "lock tailwheel" – "tailwheel locked". Sometimes the lever is quite stiff, but Mac can see when I'm struggling, gives a quick 'wiggle wiggle' with the rudder and the locking pin pops out every time. The tailwheel assembly is probably the weakest part of the whole aircraft, and as the locking pin costs $1,000 to replace (and it's specifically designed to break) Mac takes care to never stress it. Indeed, whenever we are on the ground I note that the control yoke is never aft of neutral. With the run-up and all checks complete Mac carefully lines us up and rolls forward a few metres to ensure the tailwheel is straight. I then lock it; he stands on the brakes and slowly opens the throttles to 30 inches. Even now, with the aptly-named Cyclones blasting four tornadoes of thrust across the tailplane, the yoke is forward of neutral. Brakes off and the Fort accelerates rapidly. Mac sets the throttles to roughly 40 inches and then places both hands on the yoke, leaving me to fine-tune the power. I'm a bit slow adjusting number four, and by the time I've got all the manifold pressures set at 40 inches the tail is up, the airspeed is already past 50kts and the noise is phenomenal. At about 90 I feel Mac add just a hint of back pressure to the yoke, the eager rumbling of the wheels stops and the Fort sort of waffles into the sky. Everything is very unhurried; it almost feels like an over-sized Cub.

"Positive rate". "Gear up" replies Mac, deftly stopping the still-spinning wheels. I raise the guard over the surprisingly small switch, click it forward and look out my side window. The big wheel raises itself somewhat ponderously, before half-disappearing into the number 3 nacelle. "Mine's up". "Mine too" he replies, and a glance at the undercarriage status lights on the panel confirms that the tailwheel is also safely tucked away, so I click the switch back to neutral and lower the guard over it. The speed keeps increasing and Mac smoothly eases the throttles and props back, makes a further reduction and then to the cruise setting. We've taken off with the flaps up, so all I have to do is adjust the mixtures, cowl flaps and props. I move each control slowly and deliberately, having identified it first. We both spot the B-24 at the same time, and Mac is soon easing us into formation. He's clearly working hard, and our light weight (we're about two thirds the weight of a bombed-up B-17) and the fact that we're flying relatively low and the thermals are starting to pop isn't helping, although even the bigger thermals probably don't compare to a near miss from an 88mm flak gun. Mac's eyes are riveted on the Liberator, so I dutifully scan MP and RPM, cylinder head and oil temperatures, oil and fuel pressures and the myriad other gauges. Everything's perfect, and as we close on the unmistakable shape of the B-24 I sense movement in my peripheral vision and look out of my side window across the tops of two huge prop discs.

As briefed our P-51C escort has joined up on us, and for reasons I can't fully explain it really looks good to see it there. A Mustang or two must've been a wonderful sight to a crew limping home with shutdown engines and wounded men, and I know that photographing the B-17 and its graceful guardian must be an emotional experience for photographer Jim, who is shooting from the Liberator's starboard waist gun position. His father was a B-17 pilot with the 8th AF and even flew on Black Thursday, when almost 25% of the attacking Fortresses were shot down during a catastrophic raid on Schweinfurt. Over a beer that evening he admitted that his Canon's viewfinder had unaccountably misted up once or twice.

With all the pictures in the can we move out of formation and Mac lets me fly. I try a couple of gentle turns and instantly realise it is important to lead with the rudder and that the controls are quite heavy and also not very powerful, although this may be because they're all fabric covered. It is certainly a much nicer flying aircraft than the Liberator. The handling somehow seems more positive, albeit rather ponderous. It also seems very stable - in fact it rather feels like a giant Cub. Nevertheless, it must've been very hard work to fly a heavily-laden B-17 in close formation at high altitude, through a 'diseased sky, blotchy with ugly bursts of flak'. Cruising through Florida's peaceful sky with that iconic yoke in one hand and the other resting on the throttles with the massive motors lazily loafing along is an almost surreal experience. It's also 70 years and thousands of miles from Nazi Germany, and the 'black flak and nightmare fighters' described in Randell Jarrell's powerful poem 'The Death of the Ball Turret Gunner'.

Mac indicates that we're fast approaching Zephyr Hills and resumes control while I retrieve the checklist and check booster pumps and cowl flaps, set the mixtures to 'auto-rich' and lower the flaps to 15 degrees. As we turn downwind I increase the rpm to 2100 before lowering and visually checking the undercarriage. On final Mac calls for full flap, then greases 'Nine-oh-Nine' on in a perfect 'wheeler' and tells me to slowly bring the props up to max rpm before he gently lowers the tail. Once safely chocked I regretfully ease the mixture levers forward into ICO, and as the muted thunder of our mighty engines dies away and the giant propellers slow to a stop the sudden silence is profound. As I sit there listening to the whirling diminuendo of the gyros as they spin to a stop, I am filled with a sense of enormous respect for the crews of the 'Mighty Eighth'.

I may have just flown a Fortress, but I simply can't comprehend just how terrible and horrible it must've been fighting and dying at 30,000 feet. To be sat in the seat I'm sitting in, simultaneously soaked in sweat and suffering from frostbite, while watching a good friend's aircraft vanish into a fireball, or counting the parachutes as a crew tumble from a stricken bomber. And not just do it once, but do it over and over and over again, often on consecutive days. One week, Stiles flew four missions in five days, and wrote that "it's always work, and nine hours of it on a Berlin trip knocks you flat, and if you have to drag out of the sack at two in the morning for another nine hours of the same thing, you feel like going over the hill with no forwarding address." And brave men like Stiles didn't just do it once – a combat tour was 25 missions - or until their luck ran out.

Chapter 7
Balm after the Storm

It'd been a frustrating week. I'm in the mood to fly, but all day a long procession of squally showers and squirrelly winds have kept the hangar doors firmly closed. During the last few days the 'hundreds' pointer of my single-seat Jodel Buzz's altimeter must have been swinging back and forth like a soundless metronome as the parade of lows and troughs marched across the country. Towards evening the last squall slides off towards the north and I hurry eagerly up to the airfield. Sunset is scheduled in less than an hour and I mustn't delay. As if sharing my impatience to get airborne, Buzz starts first time, and within minutes the little Jodel lifts easily into the welcoming air. The light is beginning to take on the wonderful luminescence of an early autumn evening, and I note with a twinge of regret that the leaves on the trees are already beginning to change colour. My initial track has taken me to the south, but as Buzz swings around in a great sweeping curve and heads back towards the north west I see an amazing sight — the horizon is on fire. It isn't, of course. A scientist would tell you that within the visible range of light it is the red light waves that are scattered the least by atmospheric gas molecules, and that consequently at sunrise and sunset — when the sunlight travels a long path through the atmosphere to reach our eyes — most of the blue light waves have been removed, leaving mainly red and yellow light remaining. But for me flying has always been as much about art as science, and I have rarely seen the stage of the sky so spectacularly lit. The last of the day's storms have drifted into the west, and high above the horizon great towering columns of cumulus stretch towards the stratosphere, the tops a brilliant white and looking like the crenellated battlements of some sky god's castle, while their bases are alive with colour. Red, orange, yellow and purple vie with each other as the Sun sinks. Crimson, mauve and pink; the palette for this evening's sky is truly

sublime, and I doubt if Turner or even Van Gogh could do it justice.
Entranced, I pull back the power and take up a heading that will allow me to take in the westward view over the side, as opposed to through the windscreen. The joys of an open cockpit! You wouldn't think that just a few millimetres of Perspex would make that much difference, but they do. Sometimes they make all the difference in the world. The balmy air is soft, warm and as calm as a mill pond, but 93 million miles away nuclear fusion is converting millions of tons of hydrogen a second into energy. Now golden shafts of sunlight spear through the dying cumulus and then the great glowing orb of the setting sun dips out of the bottom of the cloud. What a spectacle! It is no wonder that every ancient civilisation worshipped the sun. Call it Apollo, Helios, Inti, Ra, Suraya or Tonatiuh — the pagan in me can certainly see the attraction. If the sky was an orchestra, it is clearly approaching a crescendo — and it suddenly occurs to me that a performance as good as this deserves an encore. If I time it just right, I should be able to watch the sun set twice, so I descend to 500ft above the strip, watch — and wait. Soon the horizon bisects the red, radiant disc and I turn downwind. As Buzz slides down towards the strip the Sun's relative descent accelerates, and as the wheels touch the grass it drops below the horizon. Full

power and Buzz surges down the strip and back into the air. With the needle of the ASI nailed to Vy and the little engine pulling for all its worth we sail skyward. Success! Defying every natural law, the sun slowly rises up out of the West and back into the sky. Feeling almost childishly pleased with myself, I level off at 1,000ft and enjoy the sunset all over again. If anything it's even better this time, then once the Sun has dipped back below the horizon I turn my head and look towards the east. Just above the horizon the dark blue band of the Earth's shadow is clearly visible, while just above it a pink 'Belt of Venus' glows gently. Night is well on its way, and I reluctantly turn downwind and slowly close the throttle. As if sensing my mood the engine is as quiet as I've ever heard it, and in the deepening dusk Buzz floats gently down onto the ground. Outside the hangar I cut the engine, and for several minutes just sit there, thinking about what an amazing adventure aviation can be, and how even the simplest hop around the patch can turn into a truly memorable event. My diminutive aircraft is a simple machine made of wood and fabric, yet from its tiny cockpit I've just watched the Sun set twice, and rise in the West. Who would've guessed that a VW-powered single-seater possessed the power to re-order the Universe?

Chapter 8
Ryan ST-A

Dancing across a perfect spring sky in a graceful chandelle with the sunlight sparkling across the shining silver fuselage as the wail of the wind in the wires merges with the engine's resolute roar is pure joy. It really is a beautiful day, and a beautiful aeroplane to go flying in!

A sleek, stylish study in silver, the Ryan ST-A is undoubtedly one of the most handsome aeroplanes ever made. Although it is only illuminated by the dull light inside one of Old Warden's famed 'aeroplane sheds' it gleams, and despite being surrounded by some truly fabulous flying machines from the 1920s and

'30s still stands out. As the hangar doors slide open spring sunlight streams into the shed and this rare Ryan practically glows in the morning sun. It's almost more of a sculpture than an airframe, and where Art Deco and Solvol Autosol meet. When I say to owner Peter Holloway that the cheap plastic drip tray under the luminous cowling looks somewhat incongruous he agrees, adding that "I really should replace it with a silver champagne bucket." And do you know something – it wouldn't look out of place!

Unlike most US-built aircraft, it has an in-line engine – a configuration that never found much favour in America, with most engine manufacturers of the 1930s preferring either the Vee, horizontally-opposed or radial arrangements. The ST-A's powerplant is a notable exception, being a Menasco D-4/87 'Super Pirate'. This four-cylinder air-cooled inverted in-line engine produces 134hp at 2,260rpm and turns a Fahlin two-blade fixed pitch wooden propeller. Interestingly, although the flaps cover about 50% of the trailing edge and have five different positions they only extend to a maximum of 30 and. Shuttleworth pilot Dodge Bailey has wandered over, and observes that they "don't really do much" and speculates that they might've been more of a training aid.

Getting in is a bit of a squeeze, particularly if – like me – you don't care to miss meals. Unlike the military Ryans the ST-A's longerons are internal and, along with the oval-sectioned fuselage, make for a tight fit. With everything set I use the wobble pump to generate some fuel pressure, prime the engine using the throttle and the engine fires third swing. I quickly move the advance/retard control to about half-way and adjust the throttle until the engine is burbling quietly to itself at 800rpm. The exhaust pipes are straight and stubby, and produce a satisfyingly crisp crackle that changes to an eager bark as soon as the revs are increased. Unsurprisingly the sight of this gorgeous machine starting up has drawn a small crowd to the fence and I give them a cheery confident wave and slowly taxi out. While strapping in I'd experienced more than a twinge of trepidation - who wouldn't? However, as is often the case once the engine has growled into life the eager ruffling of the propwash soon blew away any apprehension and I taxi in a sedate series of S-turns towards runway 21. Visibility over the nose isn't great and it is prudent to taxi at only one speed – slowly! The pre-take off checks are straightforward, with the only irregularities being to ensure that the ignition control is fully forward to 'Advance' and that the fuel selector is on 'Res'. I set the first notch of flap, carefully line up and slowly bring the power

in. Keeping straight is easy, a slight swing is effortlessly corrected with a dab of right rudder and the Ryan slides into the sky.
Peter's aircraft has an extra nine horses over a stock ST-A, and although the climb rate isn't bad, it's not as sparkling as the fuselage. An original 95hp ST can't have been much fun at MAUW in a San Diego summer. Seventy-five knots seems about right, and although the view over the nose is quite good the sky round here can be busy so I weave from side to side in order to see past the long nose and scan for traffic. Even this simple manoeuvre demonstrates quite clearly the type's crisp handling and well-co-ordinated controls.
The giant airship hangars at Cardington are a very useful landmark for keeping track of my position, so I head over to the west, and at 2,000ft-ish (the altimeter really isn't that precise) level out and look about, before trying a couple of tight 360° turns in both directions. The Ryan marque has always had an enviable reputation for fine handling and the ST-A doesn't disappoint. Both the ailerons and elevators are authoritative and felt very light and smooth, even though the static friction is quite noticeable on the ground. I always like to know what the handling is like at the slow end of the speed range, so once satisfied that no-one else is around a clearing turn is swiftly followed by a couple of stalls. This produces

no real surprises, with the caveat that the indicated stall speed is slower than I'd expected. Flaps down, it finally quits flying at about 37kt, and although at the stall there's a slight wing drop (which might've been caused by the ball being out!) it's pretty benign, with adequate pre-stall buffet. Lowering the flaps only reduces the stall by a few knots, and there is very little change in pitch-trim as they go down.

Having retracted the flaps, I accelerate to around 90kt for a look at the stick-free stability. It seems to be positive in pitch, just barely neutral in roll, and practically negative in yaw. It's certainly very 'soft' directionally, possibly because there is considerable keel area ahead of the centre of gravity and this, combined with a not-especially-large fin makes the ST-A feel somewhat directionally unstable, as indeed any aeroplane with 'Sports' in its name should be. And for pure flying sport the ST-A takes a lot of beating. Its no Pitts or Extra, but by the standards of the day it must've seemed phenomenal, and there were no manoeuvres in the aerobatic catalogue of the period that it couldn't do.

The field of view really is excellent and far superior to biplanes of a similar, or indeed any, vintage. You've probably worked this out by now Gentle Reader, but the ST-A is a very special aeroplane. With taut handling, a responsive engine and plenty of the charisma and charm unique to the open cockpit wrapped up in a luminous monoplane masterpiece of burnished argent it's just fantastic, and even sounds great. The streamlined flying wires sing their own song, with the baritone roar of the engine providing the perfect counterpoint. Throw in a sunny day and what more could you ask for? The visibility is excellent, and as Cardington's huge hangars slide under the wing it almost feels as if I'm flying a time machine. These Bedfordshire skies have seen some amazing aircraft (and thanks to the Shuttleworth Collection they still do) and as I point the shapely spinner back towards Old Warden I can't help but wonder what Richard Shuttleworth would've made of the ST-A. I reckon he'd have loved it!

All too soon it's time to go home. On the way back I cruise at a comfortable 1,750 rpm, which gives 90kts IAS for a fuel flow of approximately 30lit/hr. Overhead the airfield the windsock shows that the wind has backed slightly, although not enough to make life difficult.

My experiments with the flaps have convinced me that - as Dodge implied - they're not worth monkeying with, so rather than keep swapping hands on the stick for the five different settings I elect to simply drop the lot when I'm abeam the numbers. Proceeding downwind in an orderly fashion I wait until the wingtip appears to be almost touching the threshold, then select carb heat on, throttle slowly back, trim for 75, swap hands, full flap, swap hands again, tweak the trim, pause and then turn. More by luck than judgement a nicely curved continuous base-onto-final turn produces a near-perfect 'constant aspect' approach, and I add just a hint of power halfway round to shift the aiming point slightly further into the field. The field of view all the way round is good, and as I'm flying a fairly steep approach I never lose sight of the runway, even on short final. Over the hedge! Stick and throttle smoothly back together (the throttle is almost closed anyway) and the Ryan settles slightly, the wheels feeling for the ground. There's that fleeting, floating moment and I wait for the subtle and seamless transference of weight from wing to wheel. BOING! Through a combination of the runway's slight upslope, the long-stroke undercarriage and pilot ineptitude the wheels hit the ground while the wings are still thick with lift and I'm flying again, albeit briefly. It probably felt worse than it looked, and nothing fell off – but subtle and seamless it wasn't! It rolls out straight and true, over quite a short run. Of course, as we all know landing on grass greatly deskills the taildragger, but nevertheless as the speed drops I remain ready for a swing that doesn't come. However, I suspect landing on tarmac is a much more fraught affair, and in fact the type has quite a reputation for ground looping – which is somewhat ironic, as the Ryan sales literature of the time proclaimed that 'the new tailwheel swivel lock, controlled from the pilot's cockpit, makes ground looping virtually impossible'.

For my next take-off, I leave the flaps 'up' and can't really discern any difference in performance. Now, here's a little secret; although the ST-A looks like it's moving fast when it's standing still, when it is moving it isn't as fast as it looks! A glance at the ASI shows 120mph, but something just doesn't feel right. In fact, the ST-A is fitted with what Shuttleworth's Chief Engineer Jean Munn describes as a 'salesman's static'. Basically, the position of the static port is such that it under-reads at the slow side of the speed spectrum (and thus seems to stall at a very slow speed) but over-reads at high speed. Consequently, the indicated airspeeds are both slower and faster than they actually are! A 'salesman's static' indeed!

My second landing is slightly better, which I'm relieved about as the crowd is now quite sizeable. The ST-A is really causing a stir, which is not surprising as there are more airworthy Spitfires in the UK than there are airworthy ST-As in the world; so if you want to be the star of the show then this is the aeroplane for you. It's a real scene-stealer, and

I can almost hear the clicking of dozens of camera shutters above the noise of the engine. Having climbed carefully down from the cockpit (while doing my utmost not to leave any fingerprints) I walk a few metres away and then turn to admire the aircraft one more time. It really is a gorgeous-looking flying machine and by the standards of the day has performance to match. Every sporting pilot in the US wanted one and I don't think it had a direct competitor. In the 1930's two-seat trainers fell into two distinct categories: light cabin monoplanes of between 40 to 70hp and open-cockpit biplanes of up to 220hp. Neither group was as fast or as aerobatic, and nothing else looked even half as good. Indeed, bearing in mind that most countries still had biplane fighters in frontline service in 1940, the sleek, sexy ST-A must have been a real head-turner in 1935. It continues to turn heads, 90 years later. Why? Simple; it's one of the best-looking aircraft ever made!

Chapter 9
Supermoon

The little engine gulps in the oxygen-rich air greedily and the propeller bites into the brisk, dense wind as we race down the strip and up into the sky. The cold, crisp dry air is optimising the performance of the engine and prop, and the wings are thick with lift. My little D9 Bebe has all the zip and zest of a

World War One fighter, and in mere minutes we're floating high above the Fens upon dense pillowing air, waiting for the Super Moon. A Super Moon (the correct astronomical term is perigee-syzygy; Super Moon is an astrological term and thus somewhat simplistic) occurs when a full moon coincides with its perigee, and the one on November 14 was the closest since January 1948. For some reason – quite possibly pagan – I always like to fly on dates of solar significance. Consequently, if there's an equinox or solstice in the offing and it's VFR, I'm airborne. The absence of lights (or indeed anything electrical except the magnetos) in *Buzz* makes studying astronomical anomalies a bit trickier, but with a rare perigee-syzygy forecast to rise just before sunset it was too good an opportunity to miss. Like many pilots, the moon, planets, stars and sun have always exercised a fascination on me. This might be because all of the original astronauts and cosmonauts (my childhood heroes) were aviators, or maybe it's simply because they're all part of the sky (which I look at a lot!) It may even be the initial illusion that the cosmos is quite chaotic, when in reality they can be plotted and tracked with scientific exactitude. It was the nineteenth century Prussian polymath Alexander von Humboldt who wrote "the stars as they sparkle in the firmament fill us with delight and ecstasy, and yet they all move in orbit marked out with mathematical

precision". and it was that 'mathematical precision' that was of particular interest to many early aviators. For the brave men and women who undertook the trail-blazing, long-range flights of the 1920s and 30s, the sun, moon and stars often served a more prosaic and not poetic purpose, being absolutely fundamental to navigation. In fact, it may seem incredible to today's airline pilots, but early Boeing 707s were fitted with an astrodome, and carried a navigator who knew how to use a sextant! Applying celestial navigation techniques (which have their origins as far back as 2000BC) must have been distinctly demanding while ripping through the stratosphere with a groundspeed in excess of 600kt, and shooting an adequate 'three-cornered' hat can't have been easy!
Anyway, it was well worth seeing and I'm glad I made the effort, because there won't be a bigger one until November 2034, with the biggest of the 21st century occurring in December 2052. One to put in your diaries (or maybe not). A few weeks later I was aloft again to study another interesting phenomenon. The combination of unusually high pressure and a very strong inversion was causing the smoke from the cement works at Ketton to barely clear the chimney before being squashed down and drifting slowly downwind. From *Buzz's* cramped cockpit it really was extremely interesting to study this curious singularity

from such a perfect vantage point. When level with the plume and looking through it the low sun made the countryside appear to be completely covered by a grey translucent sea, while from 1,000ft above it was even weirder. For reasons that I still don't understand the plume drifted downwind for several miles without climbing, but then turned through almost 45 degrees anti-clockwise before spreading out. At first I wondered if it was a very mild geostrophic wind that was causing the effect, but the plume didn't really appear to have gained any height over the terrain. Whatever it was, it was absolutely fascinating and truly remarkable to watch the plume as it followed every tiny undulation in the topography. It looked as if the countryside had been placed inside a giant wind tunnel. I'd always assumed the land to be fairly flat and uniform in this part of Rutland, but the smoke showed up every subtle fold and nuance of the ground in quite astonishing detail. It really was stunning, but despite my best photographic efforts I simply couldn't capture just how intricate and delicate the smoke patterns were.

For those of us lucky enough to fly it is sometimes difficult to describe to others just how amazing the unique vantage point of a small aircraft's cockpit can be. And this time of year can be particularly good, when the combination of a hard frost, crisp, clear air and a low sun can really throw subtle ground features that were hidden under the foliage of summer into sharp relief. Then, you might see something new, even though you've looked at it a hundred times! Someone once said that "Looking but not seeing is the hearing but not understanding of the eye." That's a sentiment I fully endorse, particularly when I'm exhorting the person in the front of the glider to "keep a good lookout!"

Chapter 10
Buhl LA-1 Flying Bull Pup

The view through the window in the wing root was certainly something. Far below me, the endless wastes of the Mojave spread out in magnificent disarray as my tiny monoplane continued its ceaseless climb into the burning blue of a desert sky. The altimeter needle's relentless sweep around the dial confirmed that this particular wave system was as powerful as I'd read, and as I climbed ever higher it suddenly occurred to me that this was almost certainly the highest my ancient aircraft had ever been in its 64 years, and we were still climbing! The whole situation had a slightly surreal air about it, as had my meeting with one of the Bull Pup's previous pilots earlier that same day.

The Joshua trees had been shimmering in the heat haze as the prop slowed to a stop. I undid my harness, pushed my goggles up onto my helmet and stretched, revelling in the sudden silence. At first the small Mojave airfield had appeared deserted, but then a venerable figure appeared from the shade of an antique hangar and one of the oldest-looking men I'd ever seen hobbled slowly towards my aircraft. Screwing his eyes up against the harsh glare of the desert sun, the old man squinted quizzically at the gleaming yellow and blue monoplane. Then recognition began to dawn and his leathery face slowly creased into a grin.

"This heah arr-rplane same one that old CBS newscaster used ta own?" he drawled.

"That's right" I replied, pointing at the picture painted on the starboard side of the cowling "it's Clete Robert's old Buhl Bull Pup."

"Thought so," he nodded, "ah last flew this heah Pup way back in fifty-one, when it still had the original Szekely engine." He paused momentarily, as memories of an aeroplane he had last flown many years ago slowly returned to him.

"Damn! That was the orneriest, most cussed motor ah *ever* flew behind!" He spat on the sizzling tarmac and looked pointedly at the four cylinders of the Continental A-75 protruding from the Pup's snout. "Ah sure am glad y'all got a decent motor nowadays!"

Now, having landed a vintage monoplane on a quiet desert airstrip you wouldn't usually expect that the very first person you'd speak too, even before you'd got out of the cockpit, would claim to have flown that self-same machine almost fifty years previously! But things like that happen when you fly a Bull Pup, it's a magical little flying machine.

Manufactured during the early 1930s by the Buhl Aircraft Company of Marysville, Michigan, the Bull Pup is an extremely rare aeroplane. It is also rather unusual in that it is a factory-built mass-produced single-seat sports monoplane, and another fascinating feature of the Bull Pup is that it was offered with a choice of four different wingspans! The LA-1 has a wingspan of 30ft; the LA-1A's was 28ft, and the B's 32ft. A Speedwing version of 26ft span was also designed for air racing, but few were ordered. The most popular model was the LA-1, as is Five Zero Yankee. It was built in 1931, and was the 39th one produced. As delivered from the factory it was powered by the infamous Szekely SR-3.O air-cooled three-cylinder radial.

It's a very unusual aircraft, and even getting in and out is a little bit idiosyncratic. The easiest way in is to stand on the oleos and climb in over the front of the wires, but the best way out is to walk to the back of the wing and jump down! Once ensconced in the cockpit another of the Pup's peculiarities becomes apparent; you can still see the wheels! Being a mid-wing monoplane the view directly downward would be distinctly dismal if part of the top and bottom surfaces of the wing between the fuselage and first rib were not covered with Perspex. This really neat feature is particularly useful in the circuit and certainly adds to the Pup's considerable charm. Once strapped in by the four-point harness, the cockpit is snug rather than small, and the stick and throttle both fall easily to hand. Beneath the throttle/mixture quadrant is the elevator trim winder and an almost-impossible-to-see trim indicator – the carb heat, however, is perfectly positioned just in front of the throttle.

I would say the Pup is the easiest vintage taildragger I have ever taxied, for although the brakes are very weak, the view over the nose is excellent and S-turning is not necessary. Apart from stick, rudder and trim, flight instruments and engine gauges, there's not much else to check and if plenty of wire is visible from the filler cap then you've got gas.

Acceleration is brisk and a little bit of rudder helps keep it straight because it will swing if you let it. Ease the stick forward to pick the tail up, pause, apply just a hint of back pressure and the Pup fairly leaps off the ground, eager to be back in the air.

Initial climb rate is excellent and the handling is really sweet with controls that are nicely co-ordinated and very crisp. Most aircraft of this era used cables wherever possible but the Pup uses torque tubes connected by push rods to a rocking shaft for the ailerons. Control harmony is also very good with light ailerons and a slightly heavier elevator, with the rudder being the heaviest, as it should be.

The handling is good; the push rod-actuated ailerons offering a good roll rate even by contemporary standards. In 1931 it must have seemed very lively indeed. Slow flight is interesting. With power on, it is possible to keep flying as slowly as 34 knots, but one knot slower and it stalls quite abruptly with a pronounced wing-drop

Back in the circuit, the transparent wingroots are extremely useful. When turning base and again onto final, you can throw a crisp, snappy turn and look *through* the wing for any turkeys dragging in on a three-mile final. On final it is prudent to select a faster approach speed than either the stall speed or the Pup's flight manual would suggest. For some strange reason, Buhl promulgated an approach speed that was far too slow. Consequently, several Bull Pups were lost in stall-spin accidents while landing and the type acquired an undeserved reputation for being a little bit tricky. It is not, as long as the pilot bears in mind that it has a lot of drag and a fairly low mass. If you use 1.3 or even 1.5 Vs as your approach speed, you are way on the back of the drag curve. Sixty-five knots feels about right, for as soon as the throttle is closed and the nose raised, it bleeds energy very rapidly.

In my experience, you would have to apply yourself to overrun the runway in a Bull Pup, although it will cheerfully run off the side if you let it. As with most machines of this era, it was designed to be landed into wind and consequently its crosswind limits are quite low. If the approach has been flown correctly, the Pup will softly sit down exactly where you want it to. The long stroke undercarriage actually hangs several inches lower in flight and it combines with the big, soft tyres to produce very flattering landings. Indeed, on soft sand it is almost impossible to discern the moment of touchdown. But up in the sky is where it truly belongs, for the Bull Pup is an aircraft in which the sensation of powered flight is distilled into just about its purest form.

With a pair of stout wings sprouting from your shoulders and the wind in your hair, a full 360° of visibility above the wings, and even a fair view *through* the Perspex panels in the wing roots, it's a real magic carpet ride. On one occasion, I soared the Pup in a truly phenomenal wave above the Tehachapi Mountains. As the earth fell away beneath the glowing yellow wings, I huddled down in the cockpit as the temperature plummeted. Despite the cold, I would not have missed the experience for anything. Looking out from the Bull Pup's tiny cockpit, I really did feel as if I was sitting on top of the world. I could see the snow-capped peaks of the Sierra Nevada, the parched wastes of the Mojave Desert and even the endless swell of the Pacific Ocean. For timeless minutes I floated high above the desert, awe-struck at the incredible diversity of the landscape spread out beneath me. Free from the invisible tether of a transponder and unhindered by flight plan or ATC, I truly felt that I owned the sky.

From nearly three miles high, the view was incredible, but by now the cold had penetrated every layer of my clothing and I began to think about descending to warmer levels. Completely alone, without even the artificial sense of companionship afforded by a radio, the Pup and I plunged earthwards. As the airspeed steadily increased, the streamlined flying wires quivered and sung as the Pup trembled like a living creature in a howling gale. A few hundred feet above the desert I levelled out and began to thaw out, ruminating on the previous 30 minutes.

Although a tremendously fun machine, the Pup is rather impractical, and in a way that flight summed it up. The only real reason to fly one is for the sheer euphoric exuberance of flight itself: not to go anywhere but up, and not to fly for any other reason than that the sky is always waiting, but never impatient.

Chapter 11
Boys

Can we go to the gliding club, dad?" Luckily for me I don't usually need much incentive to visit either Buckminster or Black Mountains GC's (I'm a tug pilot and Basic Instructor at both) so when my two sons Will and George decide it's a good gliding day I usually agree with them. Indeed, the school holidays have provided plenty of opportunities to spend a day up at Saltby, and the three of us invariably have a lot of fun together. On a typical day they'll both get to fly something – usually a glider or motor glider – but sometimes I'll rent the Remorquer tug so we can all fly together. When they're not flying they also enjoy riding around on the golf-cart and helping to retrieve gliders, Will sometimes keeps the log and of course when my back is turned the members feed them endless biscuits and chocolate. At the end of the day they'll sometimes ride back to the clubhouse in the double-decker bus, or one of them sits on my lap and drives the golf-cart back to the hangar while the other makes disparaging comments about his brother's driving skills. A drink at the bar or in the pub on the way home and they usually pronounce themselves well satisfied with the day, as indeed they should. In fact, I often wonder if they're aware of just how privileged they are, and wish that more children had the chance to experience such a day. Every week we hear about problems with disaffected teenagers, with some social observers pointing out that a great deal of their disaffection simply stems from the fact that they have nothing to do. Far too many greedy councils sold off playing fields to be turned into supermarkets, while swimming pools, sports centres and youth clubs are shut to save money. It's no wonder the kids are bored! If I was rich, I'd certainly set up some sort of charitable foundation to help disadvantaged teenagers enjoy a day out at a gliding club, as I've always felt that air sports can be very valuable in promoting the social, intellectual and physical development of teenagers. With gliding, we have an activity which offers both physical and mental exercise, instils pride in solo achievement, and yet is only made possible with teamwork. Soaring flight requires the practical application of lessons learned in maths, physics and geography, while even relatively mundane airfield tasks such as keeping the log can teach young people another very important lesson - learning to take responsibility.

To become a good pilot requires discipline and self-discipline, while a good day's gliding combines all the elements of a great day out - fun, excitement, exercise and adventure in the fresh air. Just what you want when you're a teenager. I read recently that a new medical problem (currently more prevalent in the US than here – but it's only a matter of time) is the increasing number of children being treated with the drug methylphenidate. It is used for conditions such as attention deficit disorder, but unfortunately (although perhaps unsurprisingly) some eventually become dependent on the drug. Of course, you may well feel that encouraging children to ingest powerful psychostimulants isn't a great idea in the first place, particularly when a 2010 study on methylphenidate indicated that the drug doesn't promote a good academic outcome. Interestingly, there is evidence that participation in air sports can actually be therapeutic for some of these individuals, resulting in an improvement in their attitude to life – and I can well believe it.

But enough of the serious stuff - back to Will and George, for as much as they like flying with me, I love flying with them. It really is a joy to see the stage of the sky through the eyes of a child, and their enthusiasm is infectious! By using George's booster seat and firm cushions Will can reach the controls, while George greatly enjoys the view – but it is their powers of observation that I find endlessly fascinating. Aviator's often talk about the advantages and pleasures of a 'bird's eye view', but until I started flying regularly with my children I'd never really thought about a 'baby bird's eye view'. They see everything. Circling round a single puffy cumulus, and looking for the 'glory' with our shadow in its centre is great sport, as is plunging into a thin, wispy cloud and then bursting out of the other side. Even a simple winch launch can generate an "Epic!" from George, while thermalling with a Red Kite last week made Will's day. Even a relatively ordinary event can sometimes create an extraordinary sight. While over-flying the airfield in the T-61 recently a powerful summer squall drenched nearby RAF Cottesmore (I still can't call it Kendrew Barracks) and then swiftly moved on. The sun promptly reappeared through a hole in the clouds and shone directly onto the rain-soaked runways and taxiways, and as practically everything surrounding the airfield was still in shadow the effect was quite remarkable – as if the runways and taxiways were streams and rivers - and William saw it first. We were still talking about it that evening.

The sights we see and share are the same sights that a million aviators have seen from a million cockpits, and yet at the same time they're unique, for no two clouds are exactly the same. And I wouldn't have it any other way.

Chapter 12
Beech 18 Expeditor

Few things are more sonically satisfying than operating the twin throttles of two well-tuned radials. As we rumble across the Berkshire countryside, owner Tim Darrah gives the port prop lever the tiniest of tweaks and then they're beautifully synced. I glance at Tim and we both grin at each other. No words are necessary – the grins are enough. Sometimes, life's a Beech!

Known variously as the Beech D-18, Twin Beech, C-45 and Expeditor, this iconic aircraft has long been on my 'wish list', so when the opportunity arose to fly one I only hesitated for a millisecond!

As Tim and I wander out to the Beech, on a beautiful autumn day at White Waltham, my initial impression is that it is quite a big aeroplane, while the US Army paint scheme gives it a wilful, almost aggressive appearance. The first thing to do is to pull each engine through nine blades to prevent any prospect of 'hydraulic lock' and after a thorough pre-flight climb into the cabin (which can carry up to eleven people) via a door on the port side, just aft of the wing.

One thing's for sure, with a MAUW of almost 4,000kg, a wingspan of 14.5m and two 450hp engines the Expeditor definitely fits the 'big taildragger' class. Consequently, I sat in the cockpit with Tim for some time familiarising myself with the controls before even thinking about starting the engines. Most aircraft of this vintage are usually ergonomic nightmares, and the Expeditor is no different. There are, buttons, knobs, levers, handles and switches everywhere - even under the seats! Just to confuse things further, both the layout of the primary flying instruments and the power control levers are completely non-standard.

Although often operated as a 'two crew' cockpit, as with most machines of this era the panel isn't duplicated left and right. Instead the flight instruments are on the port side, with the engine gauges in two central columns of three. Each gauge has multiple pointers and shows rpm, manifold pressure, oil and fuel pressure, and oil, carburettor and cylinder head temperatures. I found the engine instruments relatively easy to interpret, but the flight instruments? Forget it! As with most American aircraft of the 1940s their layout is completely non-standard and difficult to scan. The fuel system is – shall we say – not intuitive. There's only one gauge, even though there are five tanks (two in each wing and one in the nose). There's scope for real confusion here, as when you select a tank on the gauge, quantity remaining in that tank is shown in tenths. However, the front tanks are larger than the rear, so although the gauge may show the front port is 4/10ths full and the rear port 8/10ths, there's actually more fuel in the front tank. A centre console carries the power levers in a non-standard arrangement, with the prop levers nearest the pilot, mixtures nearest the co-pilot and throttles in the middle, along with levers that control each engine's manifold heaters and oil shutters, and flap and undercarriage selectors. A flat sub-panel below the console carries the fuel valves, T-handles for the tailwheel lock and park brake, plungers for oil bypass and oil shutoff, engine primer and fire suppression selectors. Two handles next to the pilot's right knee that resemble handbrakes from a vintage car operate the cowl flaps, while a large red lever by the co-pilot's left hip works the wobble pump. A big wheel on the right side of the pilot's seat operates the elevator trim, there's a small wheel for aileron trim between the flap and undercarriage selectors and a handle in the roof (which resembles a car's window winder) for rudder trim. Elevator, rudder and flap position indicators are above the columns of engine gauges, directly below the two large, red, guarded 'prop feather' buttons, and there's a red handle (which resembles a truck's window winder) in front of the elevator trim wheel to manually operate both the undercarriage and the flaps. Just like the exterior, everything is built to last. The yoke is suspended from a beam that looks like it's been borrowed from a bridge, while the rudder pedals are clearly designed for pilots who wear boots.

Finally, we get down to the business of starting a big twin-engine warbird. As has probably become apparent, starting it is very much a ritual, with a considerable number of buttons, switches, knobs and levers to be pushed, pulled, twisted, turned and set. Items that pilots of modern aeroplanes will be unfamiliar with include pushing the oil shut-off plungers 'In', opening the cowl flaps, closing the oil shutters and selecting the fire extinguisher to the appropriate nacelle. Tim starts his motor with barely a murmur – and now it's my turn, so I crack the throttle open slightly, shout "Clear prop" and energise the starter. Slowly, the big two-blade propeller begins to revolve and after six blades scythe past the window I turn both magnetos on. From within the bowels of the cowls come a cough and a grunt as a couple of cylinders fire somewhat hesitantly, then a backfire. Bugger! A few more cylinders fire and the motor begins to wake up. Smoke streams back from the exhaust and suddenly the remaining cylinders burst into life, turning the two propeller blades into a single shimmering circle and the engine soon settles into that wonderfully liquid radial rumble. I'm not really an animist, but sometimes I swear that these big old engines really do 'come to life'!

While the motors warm up I notice several people standing by the fence and give them a jaunty wave. Clearly the sound of a pair of 'Wasp Juniors' rumbling away has generated some excitement, and not just in me, for I am excited! I've been lucky enough to fly several truly iconic aircraft over the years, and although it's easy to become blasé, I'm genuinely looking forward to trying to tame this charismatic machine. However, my excitement is tinged with trepidation, as - particularly when taking off and landing – the Expeditor does have a reputation for being a bit of a handful, if not a real, 24-carat SOB (and I don't mean "son of a beech"!)

Tim eases us out of our parking spot and gives me control. Steering is by a combination of differential thrust and differential braking, so as soon as we're rolling I immediately draw the throttles back and carefully and exactly set each engine. This is important, as even a suggestion of differential thrust will make taxiing more difficult. The field of view isn't bad, but I'm still glad Tim is keeping an eye on his side.

Tim has around 25,000 hours (including about 1,000 in DC-3s) and the take-off brief is both succinct and comprehensive, and includes the procedures to be adopted in the event of an engine failure. We also review the other critical air speeds, such as the limiting speeds for the undercarriage and flaps and that a good climb-out speed

Having carefully lined up with the centreline and ensured that the tailwheel is locked, I take a deep breath then smoothly and gently open the engines up, leading slightly with the port engine to counter any tendency to swing. The engines' rumble swells to a roar, the rudders come alive almost immediately and the needle of the ASI starts to move. As the airspeed continues to build I gingerly ease the yoke forward. With radial engines swinging big props there's a great mass of metal whirling around on each wing, and gyroscopic precession is a force to be reckoned with. Pick the tail up too quickly and a swing is almost inevitable.

As the mighty motors snarl out their one-note song the Expeditor accelerates expeditiously. With 900 horses pulling eagerly the speed is surging and I can feel the wheels starting to skip as the wing takes the weight. I gently ease the yoke back, the skipping stops and we're off the ground! I check forward on the yoke slightly to stop the nose rising, as we need to accelerate "Positive rate" says Tim. "Gear up" I reply and he selects the undercarriage 'up'. we climb away with the flaps up, undercarriage retracting and the speed still increasing.
At 500ft I pull the throttles and props back to the 'max continuous' settings and set off in pursuit of the Nanchang camera ship carrying photographer Keith and Lawrence, and even at this relatively low setting the engines are still guzzling gas at a wallet-draining rate. I'm constantly jockeying the throttles, including setting the thrust up quite asymmetrically to help me hold the right position for Keith to shoot a 'head on' shot. Our vintage motors probably don't care for this sort of treatment, and out of the corner of my eye I see Tim tweaking a cowl flap here, an oil shutter there or just adding a bit of manifold heat.
We soon get the pictures in the can, and after a final spirited break we depart company with the Nanchang and I can begin to evaluate the aircraft more thoroughly. An examination of the general handling soon reveals that

although the controls are reasonably heavy they are quite effective, and even relatively steep 360° turns aren't difficult as the controls are nicely harmonised and the control authority good. Unsurprisingly the Expeditor has positive stability around all three axes, and I think it would not be too onerous to fly on instruments, as long as it was trimmed correctly. That said, scanning that non-standard panel probably isn't easy! Talking of trim, the only trimmer I adjusted was the elevators, and even then, probably less than one turn of the big wheel (it is very powerful). The field of view is pretty well what you would expect of a World War II transport. Not bad, but not brilliant. For a look at the engine-out characteristics Tim set the power so that I effectively had zero thrust (ie, replicating an engine that was shut down with the prop feathered). The performance was perfectly acceptable, but that observation must be qualified by pointing out that we were a long way below MAUW. Losing an engine just after take-off on a hot day with a full load would be seat-chompingly worrying, particularly if you'd taken off towards high ground. Slow flight is surprisingly benign, and with the flaps down and a bit of power I actually get the ASI's needle flickering just below 70, while Vne is 220kt.

All too soon it was time to RTB, and as we cruised back towards White Waltham in a gentle descent with the engines just loafing along it was easy to imagine what it would've been like flying this aircraft over the Canadian Rockies half a century ago. As with the other big piston-powered aeroplanes that I've flown it's a lot more than the sum of its parts, which are simply a disparate collection of metal, rubber and plastic. I know it's a cliché (which - as you know - should be avoided like the plague) but it's irrefutable; this thing's got soul!

Having joined overhead we wait until we're downwind, and then get busy with the flaps, cowl flaps and undercarriage before I sit up a little straighter in my seat. Now comes the real challenge – landing! As mentioned earlier the Expeditor does have a reputation, and I know it has humbled many a better pilot than me. As I level off, reduce speed and turn base I can feel myself tensing up on the controls so momentarily relinquish my grip on the yoke and then hold it slightly more loosely. I'm really concentrating and am very conscious of being entrusted with a rare piece of aviation heritage. The thing about big taildraggers is that – unlike a nosewheel aircraft, they're inherently unstable on the ground. We both know that if I cock it up, Tim will have his work cut out rectifying things. If, indeed, things can be rectified. If a real swing develops, we'll just be along for the ride! Although a swing is always lurking for any

taildragger, the twin fins and powerful rudders make the Expeditor quite controllable directionally. The big issue for a Twin Beech, and especially at White Waltham, is the bounce. I've got to pin it, or go around. Otherwise a PIO is almost inevitable.
As I bank onto final Tim lowers the rest of the flap and I draw the throttles back slightly, lower the nose and push the prop levers all the way forward. Everything's looking good. The speed, angle and sink rate are all bang on, and luckily for me the 1100 metres of runway 25 are slap into about 12kt of wind. (In fact, luck has nothing to do with it. The truth of the matter is I've been waiting weeks for today's conditions, and have cancelled two previous opportunities. I didn't fancy either of the other, shorter runways and as for a crosswind, forget it! As we slide down the slope with the speed slipping back I feel my confidence build. Good landings come from good approaches, and this is a good approach. As we sail over the hedge at exactly 80 I ease the throttles closed, check the sink rate and then let it settle gently onto the mainwheels. The actual touchdown is gratifyingly soft, but after a brief roll we hit one of White Waltham's notorious bumps and skip slightly, before settling again. I push on the yoke slightly to pin the mains on, and then sense Tim adding just a little bit more push, to get the weight firmly on the wheels.

We're down and rolling out nice and straight, but we're not stopped yet and – wary of precession – I gently fly the tail down onto the ground. I've done it, but even at the end I nearly blot my copybook, by starting to turn off the runway faster than a walking pace. "Steady" Tim cautions, and I quickly straighten up and come to a stop, then unlock the tailwheel and taxi clear of the runway. Flaps up, cowl flaps open and I turn to Tim with an enquiring "Well?" "You know" he replies in his soft Irish brogue "I doubt you'll get a much better landing than that on this runway." "In that case" I laugh, "let's quit while we're still ahead!" A bit of me desperately wants to do another couple of circuits to see if I can make a better landing, but my pragmatic side knows that this is unlikely!

Back at our parking spot those marvellous motors continue to pulse through the airframe with their deep, rhythmic throb, and with the shut-down checks complete, I reluctantly draw the mixture levers back into Idle/Cut-Off, the engines die away and the propellers slowly windmill to a stop. Tim quickly unstraps and goes aft to open the door but I'm in no rush, so just sit back, slide my window open and enjoy the peace and quiet of simply doing nothing. With a start, I realise that the back of my T-shirt is damp. I must've been really concentrating, and I had Tim to hold my hand! This is quite a demanding aircraft to operate, especially single pilot. After another couple of hours of Tim's excellent training I could probably fly it solo, but VFR on a beautiful autumn afternoon over England's leafy shires is one thing, hard IFR on a 'dark and stormy night' over the Rockies would be quite another!

As I climb out Keith wanders over and grins. "That looked OK" he offers, and I grin gratefully. Tim and Lawrence appear from behind the twin tailplane grinning broadly and I grin back. Suddenly, we're all grinning inanely at each other. What can I say? It's been a good day at the Beech.

Chapter 13
Flying out of Lockdown

I can't quite shake a vague feeling of disquiet, and I don't know why. It's far from a sinister scene - in fact it's positively pastoral. A sleepy grass strip on a gorgeous late spring evening, with a gentle Zephyr blowing straight down the middle of the freshly mown runway. *Buzz's* little engine certainly sounds happy, busily chuntering away to itself, while the needles of the few gauges are all where they should be. Oil pressure, oil temperature, cylinder head temperatures - everything is perfect. And yet the uneasy feeling persists. It can't be me. I'd flown a few days previously, making the first post-lockdown aerotow out of Saltby in the BGC's EuroFox, before transferring to the Skylark for both aerotow and winch launches, and a good soaring flight. Now, it's been many months since *Buzz* last felt the wind beneath his wings, but for all my anthropomorphism a Jodel D9 is a machine – it can't have forgotten how to fly.... Another glance at the panel confirms my initial impressions – everything's perfect and even the tachometer's needle, which sometimes vacillates +/- 100rpm either side of 1,000 - is rock-steady. Suddenly impatient, I rudder the little Jodel around into the waiting wind, open the throttle and *Buzz* surges forwards, his tiny engine shouting out a challenge to the waiting sky. A quick glance at the gauges settles it. The airspeed's already alive, the tachometer is steadily increasing past its static maximum and the Ts & P are solid. Push forward on the stick to get the tailwheel up, a dab of rudder to check an incipient swing and the wing's already starting to take the weight. Just a suggestion of backpressure on the stick and the insistent patter of the wheels suddenly stops as *Buzz* slides into the sky. Stay in ground effect until the speed swings past fifty, then gently ease the nose up into the climb. Alright! It feels as if *Buzz* has just sloughed off an old skin, and the feeling of disquiet is gone in a heartbeat. Many months have passed since we last shared the sky together but it could've been yesterday, and his broad wings already feel as if they sprout from my shoulders. The initial plan had been to stay local and get back into the groove with a few circuits, but my interest has already been piqued by some very suspicious clouds to the north-west. It's been 'waving' all day, and although the surface wind has died away considerably the winds aloft are still quite strong. While studying the synoptic chart earlier in the day I'd noted that the pressure was high and the isobars straight. It's quite remarkable how few people understand that air is a fluid, and that the atmosphere is literally an 'ocean of air'. And just like an ocean, it is very rarely flat calm – there is almost always some movement somewhere; you've just got to find it. Downwind, the azure dome of the sky is slashed by some razor-straight lenticular clouds, with their sharp leading edges accentuated by the low sun. There must be some lift around here somewhere – but where? It's not easy to work it out, mostly it seems to be barely 100ft/min or less, and at times I must make judicious use of the engine, but eventually perseverance pays off and for a couple of magic minutes *Buzz* is climbing at over 400ft/min with the engine barely ticking over. This is the best lift we find, and although some may not 'get' it, I'm delighted. I'm entranced by the beauty of the sky and intrigued by the subtle ripples of wave. At 6,200ft the needle of the VSI sags back to 'zero' and I swing *Buzz* across the sky in a great sweeping 360. The sky is mine – in fact, all mine, there isn't another aircraft to be seen. Apart from the lenticulars the cobalt cupola is completely unsullied by contrails or pollution. The visibility is exceptional and I'm sure you've noticed it too – the air is clearer, isn't it? Time expands and compresses as I float about at 6,000ft, profoundly content.

The air flowing around the cockpit is like ice-water; smooth, invigorating – and cold, but the view makes it all worthwhile. From up here it's difficult to believe that a vile pestilence is sweeping across the land. Everything looks clean, green and fresh, while the air seems to positively sparkle with the promise of another fine day tomorrow. Eventually, I roll *Buzz* up onto his wingtip, let the nose fall through and head for home. I've got tons of altitude so its trim forward and plunge earthwards. The wind and the sun are both directly behind me, so I have excellent visibility and (for a D9) tremendous ground speed. As we sail across the sky the little engine is practically singing at 3,000rpm and the yellow-painted prop tips form a single continuous ring, which looks amazing. Downwind-to-final is flown in a single flowing turn, the wing gives up the last of its lift and the wheels sink gently onto the warm, welcoming earth. It's been a long lockdown - but that flight was worth the wait.

Chapter 14
Bücker Bü 133c
Jungmeister

Barrel-rolling a Bücker Jungmeister through a superb September sky with the pulse of the engine throbbing through the throttle and the warm wind playfully tugging at my silk scarf is just too much fun. My one regret? I wish I didn't have to give it back!

It's widely accepted amongst vintage aircraft aficionados that Carl Bücker designed two of the best-handling biplanes ever made - the famous Jungmann and the fabulous Jungmeister. The Pitts Special of its day. I was genuinely excited at the prospect of flying this magnificent machine, and seeing it standing on the hallowed turf of Old Warden, knowing it was waiting for me was a thrill. Having had a full briefing by well-known warbird pilot Stu Goldspink, and a further chat with the Shuttleworth Collection's Chief Pilot Dodge Bailey, it was time to examine the machine in detail. From a distance this stubby little aircraft has a pugnacious, almost wilful look about it – but looks can be deceptive, it's actually a pussycat.

The heart of any powered aircraft is its engine – and the Jungmeister has a big heart. Tightly encased beneath the big 'bumped' cowling is a is a Siemens 'Bramo' SH14A-A4 seven-cylinder air-cooled radial, which produces up to 160hp at 2,400rpm and turns a laminated Birch two-blade propeller.

Pull the engine through at least eight blades to ensure that there's no lock while listening to the metallic 'clack' of the impulse coupler, then it's time to saddle up, sensibly attired in leather helmet and gloves, with a silk scarf accessory. Hey, if you're going flying in an open cockpit, single seat biplane a silk scarf is practically mandatory!

Strapping in is a bit of a faff, as you need to fasten the seat-type parachute. The seat adjusting mechanism is very neat – there's a lever you just twist the top of the lever to unlock it and then raise or lower it to adjust the seat. This is a great feature as you can sit up high when taking off and landing, and lower yourself down in the cockpit in the cruise, out of the wind

Starting just about any aero-engine of this vintage is something of a ritual, and is no exception. With the fuel valve set to Normal the wobble pump is... er wobbled to raise the fuel pressure, then the throttle set to 'half open' and a vigorous squirt of primer applied as each blade is pulled through. As the ignition is in the 'Retarded position' at low throttle settings, it is important not to open the throttle too much on start in order to avoid a backfire and an engine running backwards. I set the rotary mag switch to both, Peter gives the prop a healthy flip and the motor coughs, fires and lazily chuffs into life. Puffs of white smoke, accompanied by pops and bangs emanate from the exhaust until all cylinders are drawing fuel (the primer doesn't appear to charge each cylinder evenly) but gently easing the ignition forward to the 'Advanced' position makes the engine run smoothly and the black blades dissolve into a shimmering disc. Check that the oil pressure is rising nicely and then just sit back and listen while the engine grumbles away to itself with the wonderful, liquid rumble that only a well-tuned radial can produce. Once the oil is warm I set off towards the active runway with the exhaust emitting a smooth growl. There is only one

way to taxi a machine like this – and that's very carefully. my stately progress towards the runway is in a series of slow, sinusoidal S-turns, as otherwise it is simply impossible to see what's directly in front.
I line up on Runway 03 and ease open the throttle. Acceleration is good, all the controls come alive immediately and I gently pick up the tail, significantly improving the view forward. I anticipate a slight swing as the tail comes up, then just ease back on the stick and the Jungmeister leaps off the ground in around 200 metres.
Roaring skyward produces a reasonable view forward and a fair vertical velocity but the facet I'm immediately aware of are the controls. There's just so much authority in all three axes, and within seconds I know I'm at the controls of a real thoroughbred. Bückers have always had an enviable reputation for beautifully balanced controls, and the Jungmeister does not disappoint. The four ailerons are light and powerful and the elevator seems beautifully balanced. It's an incredibly impressive machine. The cockpit is warm and snug and (for a biplane) the field of view quite good.
I always like to ascertain how an aircraft handles on the slow side of the speed scale before landing it, so at a safe altitude (which coincided with cloudbase) I tried a couple of stalls. These are incredibly benign, as the

Jungmeister really doesn't want to stop flying. If you insist it reluctantly drops its nose and a wing, but simply release the back pressure and it immediately starts flying again.
Time to try a few circuits. A bit more headwind would've been nice as 03's slight downslope will exacerbate any tendency to float, so I gently close the throttle abeam the numbers and then simply fly a classic curved approach. Sixty knots 'around the corner' tapering back to a 'last look' of 55 feels about right. After half-a-dozen touch-and-goes the landings are getting quite smooth, but nevertheless it really seems to pitch, buck and rock 'n' roll on the ground run. When afterwards I ask Peter how the landings looked, he replies "fine" and explains that the springy, short-coupled undercarriage really exaggerates the bumps in the runway. It feels much worse than it looks.
The next time I fly the Jungmeister there's a fresh south-south westerly blowing right down the runway, and the Jungmeister is airborne almost before the throttle hits the stop. Climbing up into a flawless sky with the radial roaring out its wonderful song I just can't believe my luck. It's a perfect day for flying, and I'm flying the perfect machine. Climbing away to the east I briefly re-examine the primary controls and confirm my previous conclusions: for a biplane designed in the mid-1930s the handling is nothing short of

amazing. At a sensible altitude I run through checks, select aerobatic on the fuel valve, give the wobble pump a quick wobble and the harness an extra tug, and start off with a couple of delightful spins. Stall turns, chandelles, loops and rolls are all a joy – just think about a manoeuvre and it happens. Care does have to be taken on both the up and down lines, but for two very different reasons. As the prop is fixed-pitch it's quite easy to over-speed the engine in a dive (the factory red-line was 2,400rpm, but Peter has built in a safety margin by red-lining his at 2,200rpm)—while on the up-line it bleeds energy very rapidly, probably because its got more drag than a Gay Pride parade! A great confidence builder is that whatever you do, you never get anywhere near Vne.

Pulling up into a graceful chandelle and watching the sunlight and shadows slide swiftly across the taut fabric simply confirms what I'd known within seconds of leaving the ground on my first flight in it. This aeroplane really is way too much fun, and my grin feels wider than the six-metre wingspan. Time now to explore the Jungmeister's main claim to fame; the flick roll. And here everything you've read is true – this thing flicks like a demon. Add some aileron at an appropriate moment and it flicks even quicker.

A couple of stall turns followed by a delightfully slooooowww roll and a glance at the fuel indicator suggests that it's nearly time to be heading home. Suddenly a thought occurs – could I put on a respectable show in the Jungmeister? A quick 'Hell' check, chose a prominent line feature for my notional crowd-line and here we go! Enter centre stage with a three-turn spin, recover parallel with the virtual crowd line, gain some speed (watch the rpm!) and straight up into a loop, then a chandelle to the left and one to the right, more speed and a barrel roll. Start slowing down, check speed, height and rpm, then flick, recover and ease the nose down. More speed, up into a loop with a roll off the top, another flick and then exit stage left to tumultuous applause... or not. You see, the thing is that the only things I do near the ground are takeoff and land. Consequently, although my little routine might've been quite good (and it certainly seemed perfectly respectable) as I never went below 2,000ft any airshow punters would be demanding a refund.

Another glance at the float suggests that it's definitely time to be heading home, so it's select normal on the fuel valve, a quick wobble of the wobble pump and start searching for Old Warden. Cruising back towards the airfield with that lovely round motor rumbling away (it's one of the smoothest radials I've ever flown behind) and a waterfall of warm air flowing around the cockpit is simply wonderful.

Back in the circuit, I'm determined to get it right for my last landing so I concentrate on the numbers, and the second I'm abeam them slowly close the throttle, ease the elevator trim back and immediately commence turning in, intending to go from the downwind leg onto short final in one great sweeping curve, the way aeroplanes like this should be flown. Due to the blustery wind, I use 65/60kt, and with the wind sighing in the wires the Jungmeister comes floating over the fence. All the speeds and angles are bang on, and as we cross the threshold with just a hint of power on I begin easing the stick back. It all feels just right... and, you know, it very nearly is. The bulbous nose slowly rears up, completely obscuring the forward field of view, but my confidence is up and my peripheral vision firmly focused. With a barely a bump the wheels settle onto the grass, just past the numbers and right on the centreline. But it's been six weeks since my previous flight, and I've forgotten how much the oleos extend in flight. Instead of a perfect three-pointer the mains touch first and there's a slight skip before the Jungmeister settles gently onto the ground. Bugger.

Back at the pumps I switch the mags off, the glorious rumble dies away and the prop lazily huffs over the last couple of compressions and stops. In case you haven't guessed by now, I really like the Jungmeister; it's a fascinating contradiction of a flying machine, in that despite the (for its age) sparkling performance and crisp handling, the low wing loading means that it doesn't have any vices or vicious traits, and is actually quite easy to fly. It's fantastic in the air, while the steerable tailwheel, toe-operated brakes, large rudder and four ailerons make it very tractable on the ground too. It also just oozes bags of charisma. What a truly magnificent machine!

Chapter 15
Flying for Free

As I look out of my window at a flawless blue sky the weather forecaster on the radio is talking about the 'Polar Plume' that is extending down from the North and bringing with it 'a blast of Arctic air'. It was almost zero last night and is forecast to hit 12°C this afternoon, and I don't need a Master's in Meteorology to know that this temperature spread combined with the passage of a cold front will produce spectacular soaring conditions. It's clearly a day to be in a sailplane, but having only just returned from flying a PC-6 and PC-12 in Switzerland and with a trip to Vienna scheduled for later in the week the work is piling up and I simply don't have the time for a day's gliding. However, that doesn't mean I can't go flying, and as I pull *Buzz* out of the barn I suddenly have an idea – why not glide anyway? If I fly *Buzz* as if he were a sailplane, it should be an interesting exercise to see just how little fuel he can burn in an hour. So, I carefully fill the tiny tank to the brim, finish the pre-flight – and wait. Although the sun is warm the air is cold, but being dressed for flight I'm quite cosy. There isn't a breath of wind so it's all very agreeable to simply lay back on the grass and listen to the birdsong. The stainless sky is ice-blue and unblemished by even a single cloud. I wait. After about an hour there's a sudden rustling in the trees and the grass cuttings scattered across the strip are snatched off the ground and go whirling up into the sky. The temperature has reached the trigger point, and thermals are beginning to form! Flip the tiny prop, the little motor jumps joyously into life and within minutes we're rushing wide-winged into the welcoming wind. Climbing away from the strip *Buzz* is already being rudely jostled by the bubbles of warm air breaking away from the surface. At about 750ft *Buzz* starts to tremble, there's a sudden surge under my seat and the VSI's needle swings up. I reef the little Jodel round in a tight turn, whip the trimmer back and gently reduce power to about 2,400rpm, or 1,000rpm below the 3,400 red line. The altimeter is winding up at a gratifying rate while the VSI occasionally touches the 1,000fpm mark. This is a strong thermal! As we spiral skyward I pull the throttle back a bit more and then wind the friction up tight. It is my intention that - if at all possible - the next time I add power it will be to taxi clear of the strip. I suddenly realise that the visibility is not just good, it is exceptionally good, and I can already see The Wash. Passing through 1,500ft I spot on the south-eastern horizon a peculiar dark grey smudge, as if someone has taken a piece of charcoal and drawn a horizontal line where the sea meets the sky. Incredulously, I do a comedy double-take. It can't be – but it is! What I can see is the north Norfolk coast, and I've never seen it from such a low altitude before. The visibility is stupendous. At about 2,500ft I fall out of the side of the thermal, and can't seem to find it again. There still isn't a cloud in the sky, so as there's no clue as to where to go I simply point the shapely spinner due north, trim forward and confidently set off. Five minutes later though I'm feeling a lot less confident. The altimeter has fallen back to barely a thousand feet, and my left-hand worries dejectedly at the throttle's knurled friction ring. Is the Great Soaring Adventure about to stop before it truly started? Suddenly there's life in the air and the port wing rises of its own volition. Stick and rudder together, there's a colossal upwelling of lift and we're surging skyward again. This is more like it! Round and round we go, with me grinning like an idiot. Unexpectedly a strange odour invades my open cockpit and I tense involuntarily. Something smells – is it hot oil? My eyes flash to the gauges but everything looks normal. Perplexed I look over the side – and laugh out loud when I realise I'm directly above a frozen chip factory.

Within minutes I top out at 4,000ft, and look around. The view is breath-taking; - I can clearly see both Norfolk and the Peak District, and even the cooling towers at Ferrybridge power station -and its 60 miles away! The air is like ice – bracing, invigorating - and freezing! Eventually, I start to drift down towards the strip and – although I intend to land - at 800ft I blunder into a massive thermal. It is so powerful I actually flinch, then instinctively turn into it. Within two turns I'm centred – and I can't ignore one as good as this. The altimeter soon reads 4,500ft, and as it's 1300 BST the sun is directly overhead and the incredible visibility makes the view match the map in a way I've never seen before. It really is quite remarkable, but I'm also extremely cold!

Thirty minutes later I'm back on the ground and thawing out in the warm spring sunshine. As planned, I only advanced the throttle twice - on takeoff and when taxying back to the barn. Carefully I refill the tank, one litre at a time. It takes less than eight litres – and I was airborne for well over an hour. Flight using the atmosphere as your fuel and your intellect as the engine – you can't beat it!

Chapter16
Fieseler Fi 156 Storch

Well, what do you think, Dave?" asked proud owner Peter Holloway. "I've gotta say, Pete" I replied, having studied the ungainly undercarriage, inverted engine and wonderful wing, "it looks like a real contraption!" Peter laughed delightedly. "You know," he grinned down at me from the Storch's tall cockpit, "*contraption* is an excellent description. Climb on up and I'll show you around..."

Almost straightaway, what really caught my eye was the sheer quality of the restoration. Every stencil is not only in exactly the right place, but even uses the correct font as well.

When I asked the purpose of the small box built into the door, Peter explained that it was for the pilot's flares. "I don't wear 'em" I replied.

Getting in is a bit of a game; it's a real climb up to the cockpit and if you're checking the fuel, you might get vertigo, you're so high up. A further complication is that although there appears to be lots of things to step and hold onto, quite a few of them are placarded 'Nicht anfassen' (don't touch) and Nicht betreten ('don't step on'). Finally, you must negotiate the floor-mounted control lock.

Once in the pilot's seat I was surprised that neither the seat nor pedals appeared to adjust. (In fact, the pedals do, but not easily). The cockpit is typically Teutonic, and features a considerable amount of colour-coding for the various instruments and systems. It is also glazed so extensively that the initial impression is of sitting in a small conservatory that has inexplicably been fitted with wings. The very high quality of the restoration has been carried over into the cockpit. The original pull-down sunshade is still installed, and the pull-out map light not only still works, but the cable is the same length as the original. This allows the light to extend out to the wing, for pre-flighting at night.

For my first flight I sat in the back, and as this is where the observer sat there are no controls at all. So I simply observed – and learnt – a great deal.

During our brief flight he demonstrated the Storch's truly astonishing slow-flight capabilities. Indeed, at one point we seemed to be practically "kann auf der stelle drehen", as they say in the Fatherland. During the briefing Peter told me that the Luftwaffe had laid field telephone cables using Storchs, and as we lazily S-turned oh-so-slowly above the fields I could certainly see how viable it was.

He also demonstrated some very flat turns using rudder only, which I didn't really care for. In fact, it really was a most disconcerting sensation, being quite low, very slow and yawing significantly.

After a very smooth landing we swapped seats, and with Peter providing me with plenty of sound guidance I wound the flaps down. The take-off and initial climb went well until I inadvertently raised the flaps too much and too quickly and we sank slightly as the pitch trim changed.

It should be borne in mind that in the 60 seconds it takes to climb 400ft you're almost certainly still within the airfield boundary, due to the slow forward speed. Throw in a decent headwind and the climb gradient is positively precipitous. Initial impressions? It's pretty slow, rather hot and quite noisy.

Once we were clear of Old Warden I began to examine the general handling. The Storch's ungainly appearance belies a surprisingly sprightly roll rate, while it was easy to keep the turns coordinated using the powerful rudder. As I swung the Storch through a series of increasingly steep turns, Peter sensed my mood and observed "You're enjoying this, aren't you?" "It's fantastic," I agreed. "After all, it isn't every day that I get to fly a piece of history!" And I really was enjoying it. It's a fabulous aircraft to fly, with an extremely good field of view.

Having convinced both Peter and myself that I could fly the Storch reasonably well, all I had to do now was land it. Unsurprisingly, it has a fairly low sink rate, and it is inadvisable to completely close the throttle as you descend, as the retarded ignition could cause plug fouling. The trick is to descend just below the glidepath, and then use just a trickle of power all the way in.

It felt like I was rather high as I rounded out, so I waited until I was sure the wheels must be almost touching the grass (although it still seemed too high) then simultaneously closed the throttle and pulled the stick right back. Obediently, the Storch simply sat straight down and rolled to a stop very quickly.

To prove to Peter that it wasn't a fluke, I flew another circuit, this time ensuring that after take-off I left the flaps down until I had 90km/h, and then retracted them in stages. On final I wound down the full 40° of flap, carried a little more power into the flare and once again it sat down exactly where I wanted it too. And one thing's for sure – with 40° of flap hanging down there's no chance of overshooting!

After lunch, I strapped myself back in, keenly aware that I was about to solo probably the finest and most authentic airworthy Storch in existence. A deep breath, and I began to run through the start sequence. First, various circuit breakers need to be pushed in, including (unusually) one for the starter. Having ensured that the throttle was completely closed (this automatically retards the ignition), I selected 'P1' and operated the wobble pump on the right side of the panel until I got an indication of fuel pressure, then opened the priming tap and gave the engine several squirts. Mags to M1 + M2, a shout of '"Propeller frei!"' (well, I was trying to stay 'in character') and I pressed the guarded starter button. The Argus stumbled into life and I checked the oil pressure, closed the primer cock, tripped the starter's circuit breaker and was ready to roll. Taxying out I noted that I had to occasionally dab the brakes to keep the speed down. You don't want the throttle set too low, as with the ignition retarded below 800rpm there's the risk of fouling the plugs. Of course, you don't want to taxi too fast either. Apart from this, it's very straightforward to taxi. The brakes are good and (for a vintage taildragger) you have a fine view. However, there are some potential 'gotchas', including inadvertently overstressing the rear fuselage when taxiing, turning and running up. This is because the tailwheel is always under considerable load, due to the forward position of the main undercarriage. Peter recommended keeping the stick central, even for the run-up. The big flaps also need to be 'up' when taxiing, as there is a risk of being rolled over in a strong crosswind. Other checks included setting the flaps, winding the trimmer to '+1 nose down', selecting the fullest tank and 'P1+P2' to ensure an adequate flow of fuel (adrenaline flow being more than adequate).

The acceleration was noticeably better without Peter's 100kg (no offence, mate) as was the climb rate. Nevertheless, the VSI remained uninspiring, and I can readily believe that in service Luftwaffe pilots exploited thermals whenever possible. As on my previous flight, the needle of the CHT was soon climbing ominously towards the red line, so I throttled back to around 1,650rpm and lowered the nose to get some more air moving through the cowling. Moving into formation with the cameraship R44 I remained acutely aware of the CHT needle's close relationship with the red line, and took care to always move the throttle very slowly. With all that glazing and a considerable amount of heat coming back from the engine it wasn't only the Argus that was getting warm, but eventually Peter announced that Damien was satisfied and we returned to Old Warden. On the way back I examined the control and stability, and confirmed my initial assessment that it is essential stable about all three axes.

Slow flight is simply as incredible as you'd imagine. Indeed, with the big flaps hanging down and some power, the wing retains such a tenacious grip on the airflow that the needle of the ASI sinks off the scale. Turning final I knew that Peter was critiquing my approach, as the R44 was in my "4 o'clock". Luckily I made another smooth landing and with Peter's "nice job, Dave!" ringing in my headset, I cleared the runway, wound the flaps up and taxied back in.

In conclusion, I was hugely impressed by the Storch. In many ways it's an excellent example of "function over form" (hey – nobody ever said it was pretty), and even by today's standards its Short Take Off and Landing (STOL) performance is remarkable. Seventy-five years ago it must have been truly astonishing. I flew it on a flat-calm day and was amazed at how little runway I used, and this was the first time I'd ever flown one. I would imagine that with few hours on type, and say 20kts on the nose, you could land practically anywhere.

In fact, while discussing flying the Storch with 'Winkle' Brown, he delighted in telling me that when he landed one on the aircraft carrier *HMS Triumph* he practically hovered onto the deck, touching down and stopping on the aft lift! He also told me that the original POH contained the phrase 'Auch der Storch ist nicht narrensicher' (Even the Stork is not foolproof). That may well be the case, but it is astonishingly capable. It performed sterling service from the frozen wastes of the Russian steppes to the scorching sands of the African Desert, and was as important to the Luftwaffe as the Me109 or Ju88. Having flown one, I can certainly see why.

Chapter 17
Rhapsody in Blue

I suppose you're going to the big 'End of Season' Ball in London?" enquired my hangar neighbour. "Eh – what's that?" I replied. "It's a big posh dance with food and.." "I know what a ball is" I interjected testily "but what is this 'End of Season' of which you speak? I fly all year round!"

I've never understood the concept of a 'Flying Season'. True, there are far fewer flying days in the winter, but the good days can be truly great. It doesn't matter if you're flying something powered by an afterburning turbojet, Merlin V-12, Continental A-65, VW-1600 - or even nothing at all, that cold dry air not only makes the engine and propeller more efficient, but even the wings can lean that little bit harder on the air. And when a cold front has swept down from the north, bringing with it a healthy Arctic airmass, then the conditions can be glorious.

It was with just these thoughts in mind that I scurried to the airfield early one morning recently. The front had gone through around dawn, and the frosty air positively sparkled with the promise of some fine flying. A smart flick of *Buzz's* propeller, the motor leaps into life and (swaddled in myriad layers of cold-weather gear) I wedge myself into the tiny open cockpit and am soon rushing wide-winged into the welcoming wind. In the cold crisp air *Buzz* is airborne after a ridiculously short ground run and soars skyward at almost 1,000fpm. This is real flying! The wind is from the northwest and as the synoptic chart indicates that it might wave I climb away to the north and search for signs of atmospheric activity. Abeam the abandoned 'airfield in the woods' at North Witham I notice that a thin, almost imperceptible bar of wispy cloud has formed, perpendicular to the wind. Senses heightened I turn to parallel the cloud, reduce power and tighten the throttle friction, then retrim until the VSI has settled on zero at a steady 60kt, take my hands and feet off the controls – and wait. A glance down at the various flight and engine instruments and it seems as if the white pointers have been painted onto the black-faced dials. Even the tachometer's needle, which usually has a 10rpm 'nervous tic', is steady. The air is so smooth it feels as if I am taxiing slowly across a frozen lake. The seconds tick by but the pointers stay still. Then out of the corner of my eye I see the VSI's needle flicker and then start fluttering weakly just above 'zero', then the 'hundreds' pointer on the altimeter slowly starts to rotate. I *am* climbing! As I begin to ascend into the wave (well, more of a ripple to be honest) the VSI shows a steady 200fpm. Now, this may not seem like much but remember I haven't adjusted any of the controls, yet am still climbing. Is it magic? It certainly seems like it! Ten minutes later the altimeter stops at just over 4,000, the VSI sinks back to zero and the view is incredible! Although the seat is simply a bit of Dynafoam Velcroed to a sheet of plywood, today it is the throne of my 'sky kingdom' and in sheer delight I swing around in a great sweeping circle and begin to drink in the incomparable scenery. The visibility is remarkable; I can see The Wash and possibly even the faint outline of the north Norfolk coast. As I gaze around a bright flash in the sky catches my eye. The sun is still so low that the airliner high above is 'bottom-lit', and as it drags its pearlescent wake across the vaulted dome of the cobalt sky I suddenly realise just how many shades of blue I can see. Directly overhead it's a very dark hue, but as I lower my gaze and look up, down and across sun I can see azure, cerulean, indigo, sapphire...It's fantastic - but the cold is starting to penetrate my flying suit, so rather than turn blue myself I roll *Buzz* onto a wingtip and dive down towards Rutland Water. The low sun is directly behind it, making the giant lake look as if it is filled with molten gold. It's quite surreal, and rather odd to think that two villages lie beneath the surface, with only the picturesque church of St Matthew's remaining on the southern shore. As I drop lower and draw nearer the houses in the tiny Rutland villages almost seem to be huddled together for warmth on this frosty morning, while the yachts on the lake look like toys. At 500ft I level out and turn towards Grimsthorpe Park. At this altitude the air is noticeably warmer and as I cross the park's boundary the tree-lined rides look incredible. Serried rows of Ash, Beech, Hawthorn and Oak all stand out in stark relief, while the leaves' myriad shades of red, green and brown look astonishingly colourful. People may go on about New England in the fall, but on the right day Old England in the autumn takes some beating. A feather-light three-pointer back at the strip wraps up a perfect flight, and I'm thawing out back at my desk by eleven and writing about the flight for my monthly column. While waiting for the coffee and computer to warm up I fill in my logbook and note with some satisfaction that during the previous 30 days I'd flown on 14 of them.

As I said earlier, I don't really understand the concept of a 'Flying Season'.

Chapter 18
Schleicher ASK-6E

The idea for this piece came from a highly-experienced test pilot with whom I flew during the 2005 AOPA Expo. Having concluded the post-flight de-brief, we were winding down by swapping a few flying yarns. A former US Navy fighter pilot and Top Gun graduate, he'd flown some very potent aircraft, including the F-4 Phantom and F-14 Tomcat. When I asked him if there were any particular types that he'd always wanted to fly, he replied that the two fighters he'd love to have a go in were the Spitfire and the Harrier. Casually, I mentioned that I had been lucky enough to fly both a Spitfire TR.9 *and* a Harrier T.10, amongst hundreds of other types. Suitably impressed, (which had been my intention all along) he suddenly asked: "Damn, boy, what do you fly on your days off?" "Ah," I replied smugly, "I own an example of possibly the sweetest-handling sailplane ever made – the K-6E".

Designed by Rudolf Kaiser and produced by Alexander Schleicher GmbH (hence ASK-6) it was a real 'hot ship' when it first appeared more than 40 years ago. Although many other sailplanes may have surpassed its performance in the last four decades, in my opinion its handling characteristics can still be held up as coming very close to 'ideal'. The ailerons are delightfully light, the all-flying tail powerful, and the rudder well balanced. However, no flying machine is perfect, and it's fair to say that the all-flying tail does have a predilection for exacerbating Pilot Induced Oscillations particularly when being aerotowed.

In common with most other aircraft designed to fly *upon* the air, as opposed to *through* it, the predominant materials in its construction are those used in the earliest flying machines – wood and fabric. The fuselage is a wooden semi-monocoque structure covered with plywood, while the cantilever wing uses a

single spar of pine and plywood, covered with fabric.
The undercarriage consists of a fixed unsprung monowheel and a steel tailskid, while the wheel brake is simply a crude band, made from the same kind of material as a conveyor belt. This is stretched across the top of the wheel when the airbrake lever is pulled fully aft. To be honest, it produces more noise than retardation!
As delivered from the factory, it was fitted with a single offset combination (compromise is a better word!) hook but 433 (in common with most K-6Es) has been retrofitted with a dedicated aerotow hook just below the nose cone. This makes the aircraft much more pleasant to aerotow, and also reduces (but does not prevent) the propensity for PIOs on tow.
Aesthetically, I find the design very pleasing – indeed, it sometimes occurs to me that it almost looks like a child's idea of what a glider should look like.
After a thorough pre-flight inspection and a positive check of all the control connections, it's time to go flying. The canopy removes completely, which makes it a bit easier to climb into the snug cockpit. However, before getting in it is important to adjust the rudder pedals, as this is tricky (though not impossible) to do once you're in. It is also necessary to wear a parachute, as the seatpan

was designed to accommodate a 'chute. A small but fascinating feature is the diminutive metal ring attached to the bulkhead behind the pilot's left ear. This ring is for attaching your parachute's static line, should it be so equipped with one. (I've never actually seen this type of parachute, and can only assume it was one of those ideas which, while good in theory, was perhaps less satisfactory in practice).

The K-6 is very much the kind of aircraft that you put *on,* as opposed to get *into,* and once strapped in with the four-point harness, you really feel as if you're 'wearing' the aircraft. The seat is very firm, so I use a sheet of energy-absorbing Dynafoam as a cushion. As the cockpit is quite small, it's important to be comfortable as there's not much room to wriggle.

The instrumentation of 433 is completely in character with the rest of the aircraft, being very simple and uncluttered. In fact, the instrument panel carries only a colour-coded airspeed indicator, altimeter and compass, along with an electric Turn & Slip and two variometers (one pneumatic and fitted with a MacCready Ring) and the other electric.

All the (very few) controls are easy to see and reach. The stick is curved in an 'S' shape and falls easily to hand, while the blue airbrake lever and yellow cable release handle are logically located. The pitch trim is adjusted via a small lever topped with a green knob mounted directly in front of the stick. The pitch trim system is a spring trimmer, which, as the name implies, is simply a large spring, one end of which is attached to the floor and the other to the stick. Moving the lever forward or back biases the spring tension in the same direction. It is held at the desired setting by tightening up a friction wing nut on the side of the lever.

Once launched, the trim is adjusted for the soaring conditions. If ridge-running down low I'll generally use 50kts, although I'll knock five knots off if the air is smooth or once I gain some height. I normally use 40-45kt when thermalling or in wave. If the opportunity arises, I quite enjoy taking the odd cloud climb, as 433's Turn & Slip works well and I always appreciate the chance to practise my 'partial panel' skills with some 'needle, ball and airspeed' work.

When moving between sources of lift there is little to be gained at flying at speeds much in excess of 75kt as the glide angle is so steep. The aircraft also has a distinct tendency to pitch up at high airspeeds and as the spring trimmer cannot compensate, the stick forces in pitch can get uncomfortably high. On the slow side of the speed envelope the stick forces are so low as to be almost unnoticeable, while the stall itself is very subtle and gentle. There is practically no pre-stall buffet, the best

indications of an imminent stall being the stick position and the change in the sound of the air flow.
The glider spins well and recovers promptly as soon as the correct control inputs are applied. It is cleared for aerobatics, but I tend not to indulge in such vulgarities. It's been designed for soaring, not aerobatting. Overall, it's a delightful aircraft to fly, with crisp, well-balanced controls, but when the conditions are lively you tend to get bounced around a bit and then it requires a firm hand. In smooth conditions I tend to let 433 fly itself. I'm a 'low gain' pilot (some might also rather unkindly describe me as lazy) and prefer not to do too much unless it's absolutely unavoidable. I tend to guide it rather than fly it.
Visibility is quite good by the standards of the day, but less impressive when measured against more modern sailplanes. Ventilation is adequate – there is a fresh air vent above the instrument panel and, of course, the DV panel can also be opened.
Landing a K-6E is as undemanding as every other aspect of the aircraft. The airbrakes supply adequate approach control, although it is important to remember to ease off the backpressure on the airbrake lever just before touchdown, otherwise you land with the brake on. The unsprung monowheel ensures you're in for a rough ride if the ground is bumpy, but the ground run is generally short.

I've enjoyed some superb soaring in 433, but one summer's evening flight in particular perhaps sums up just what a wonderful machine it is. The wind was from the northeast and the synoptic chart had indicated that it might well wave, although all day long the thermals had prevented a wave forming. I'd taken the last launch of the day, and had released into reliable ridge lift on the east face of Mynnd Troedd. After about 30 minutes of patrolling back and forth along the side of the mountain, I noticed that a thin, wispy cap of cloud had formed over the middle of the Cwmdu Valley. Now that the convective activity had at last died away, it looked as if the wave was finally beginning to form. All I had to do now was reach it! Well, after about 45 minutes I'd got nowhere fast and was still 'stuck on the hill'. I'd press out from the ridge lift as far as I'd dare and then, when I failed to contact the wave, had to do a smart 180 and run back to the hill. Here, using the dependable ridge lift I'd regain all the height I'd lost and then make another foray out over the valley.

I repeated this procedure several times, and achieved nothing. As can so easily happen, my frustration with the lack of progress drew me further and further away from the safety of the ridge as I chased the elusive wave. Consequently, when I suddenly realised I was getting dangerously low over some very small fields and that I'd better turn and run back, I was already in a pretty marginal situation and arrived back at the mountain well below the top, where the lift was a lot less consistent. After several sweaty minutes of working odd scraps of lift, I managed to claw my way back up the mountain and into the lift proper. With my position once again secure, I took a drink from my water bottle and reviewed the situation.

I'd been at this for almost an hour now, and all I'd really achieved was to give myself a good scare. The cloud cap was still there – tantalisingly close, and yet apparently unreachable. What to do? I reluctantly reached the conclusion that I had to 'go for broke' and gamble everything on one last roll of the dice. I'd get as high as I could and push out over the valley one more time. If it didn't work, I'd run straight back to the airfield, planning to join close in on a right base. So out I went again but bolder this time and, as is often the way, managed to slip into the bottom of the wave. The lift was so weak that initially I wasn't even sure if I was actually climbing. The air was so smooth that it felt like ice, so having trimmed for the minimum sinking speed I gently turned until I was directly into wind and then took my hand off of the stick. I've always maintained that 433 flew better when I wasn't interfering, and with the nose slap into wind and the glider trimmed

so that the airspeed exactly matched the wind speed (and thus the groundspeed was zero), there wasn't anything for me to do anyway.
The needle of the variometer was fluttering weakly just above 'zero', and I felt that I was balanced on the edge of a razor and didn't dare move. In fact, I was barely breathing. But when after a couple of minutes I gently tapped the instrument panel, the 'hundreds' pointer on the altimeter abruptly jumped up by a hundred feet. I *was* climbing! As I began to ascend into the wave proper, the vario began to show a steady 'two up' (two knots of vertical speed, or 200ft/min). By the time I was passing through 3,000ft this had turned into a solid 'four up' and I'd had to increase my airspeed by ten knots to prevent drifting back in the increasing wind.
Passing through 5,000ft I turned the radio on and announced smugly, "Talgarth base, four three three is established in wave over the Cwmdu, climbing through 5,000 feet, four up". To be honest, the call was more for the benefit of all the other gliding clubs in England operating on the same frequency. As it was a Friday evening, many other clubs would still be flying, but as the thermals had died away and very few gliding sites offer soarable conditions in an east or north east wind, I was quite confident that I was the only glider pilot for hundreds of miles who was actually soaring. As the (then) manager of the

Black Mountains Gliding Club, I never missed a chance to 'plug' it!

With plenty of height to play with, I relaxed and began to drink in the incomparable scenery of the Brecon Beacons national park. It was simply stunning – and as the only pilot soaring in the area it was all mine. In sheer delight I swung 433 around in a graceful, sweeping circle, and everywhere I looked was beauty. I could see the brooding bulk of the Black Mountains and the Malvern Hills, the silver ribbon of the Severn flowing into the Bristol Channel and beyond that the outline of the north Devon coast. As the turn continued Llangorse Lake came into view, with the imposing peaks of the Beacons in the near distance and Cardigan Bay beyond them.

It was magical, and although I've never been an animist (which is why I tend to refer to 433 as 'it' and not 'she') I remember affectionately patting the side of the cockpit and thanking 433. Why? Well, I really think I couldn't have done it in any other type of glider. I wouldn't have fancied scratching so low on the mountain in anything else, while I needed the slow speed and low sink rate to get into the bottom of the wave. What a wonderful sailplane!

Chapter 19
Summer Solstice

The early morning Solstice sky is flawless. As blue and clear as a tropical sea, and as immense and serene as space itself, it promises a fine day's flying and I eagerly open the hangar door. There's something about pulling your own personal aircraft out of the shed on a fine summer morning that just feels great, and it feels even better when it starts first swing!

A warm zephyr is blowing gently down the strip, and as the throttle hits the stop the little aeroplane bounds forward with the slipstream battering the windscreen. The far hedge is no longer as far as it was, but suddenly the urgent pattering of the wheels stops, the wings take the weight and my Jodel D9 *Buzz* slides smoothly into the sky. With every hundred feet of altitude my world-view expands, and soon I can see three different counties, a giant lake and half-a-hundred other interesting sights. It never grows old.

I climb away from the delightful grass strip where *Buzz* lives and set course for Saltby airfield, where a fun day's flying awaits. At the Buckminster GC we have a long and noble tradition of flying as much as possible on the Solstice, and there is always a group of hardy pilots (not me, obviously – if I have to be up at 0400 I probably wouldn't bother going to bed) who like to launch at dawn and into dusk. I plan to spend several hours there helping out, and flying anything that needs flying.

Having landed and partaken of a free bacon roll (part of the allure of arriving reasonably early on the Solstice) I help out at the launch point for a few hours while revelling in some cracking banter and simply enjoying being out in the sunshine with fine flying machines and good people. Eventually the Duty Tug Pilot indicates that he wouldn't mind a break, so I hop in the old Remorquer for half-a-dozen tows. This is good fun, but I've already spotted that the club's Schleicher K-8 has been on the ground longer than is good for it – and as soon as the Duty Tuggie has been fed and watered I strap on a chute, slip into the cockpit and am hooked up for a winch launch. Being a little rusty 'on the wire' I only get an average launch and don't really expect to get away, but luckily a giant thermal grabs my little glider and within minutes I'm at 4,000ft! Can the day get any better? Yes! Some suspicious-looking clouds to the East herald a rare sea-breeze front, and the lift is superb. As the front passes over the airfield the wind swings right round and I watch as the entire operation (coach, winch, tug, cars and gliders) swap ends. After a delightful flight I land the K-8, hop into *Buzz* and am meandering back to base through a pellucid evening sky when the amazing adventure of aviation suddenly strikes me. Here I am, thousands of feet in the air in a home-made machine built mostly of wood-and-fabric and propelled through the air by an engine that was designed in the 1930s - for a car! Indeed, with its open-cockpit and raucous exhaust flying in *Buzz* is reminiscent of the Golden Age of Aviation, when all aircraft were wood-and-fabric. Sunlight and shadows slide across the wings as *Buzz* hums homeward and the little engine sounds as content as I feel. Having extracted some extra energy from the last evening thermal I'm considerably higher than necessary, so with a grin nudge the trim lever forward and slalom down through the sky in a series of sinuous S-turns. I'm not exactly sure what constitutes ‘poetry in motion’ but sweeping through the sky like a toboggan on the Cresta Run works for me! Abeam the downwind hedge I turn through 180 in a single graceful curve and roll the wings level on short final. An ephemeral moment of buoyant floating, then the gentle rumble of all three wheels tells the tale of a textbook three-pointer. Cut the engine outside the hangar and the sudden silence is profound – almost unreal. As my hearing slowly returns to normal I become aware that – far from being silent -the air is full of sound. There’s birdsong, a chugging tractor, a yapping dog and a distant train.

As I roll *Buzz* back into the shed I pause and pat his spinner affectionately. Its been a good day, and in a world of over-regulation, hypocrisy and selfishness it was a joy to see a British gliding club at its best. A safe yet slick operation (69 glider launches plus lots of motor glider movements and an itinerant D9) a minimum of bulldust and – best of all – a fine group of like-minded people having some fun and exercise in the fresh air while putting in more than they take out. For from the instructors and tug pilots, via the log keepers, winch drivers and bacon-butty makers - absolutely no one was getting paid. And to me that’s the essence of air sports; everybody contributing for one simple reason - because they love to fly.

Chapter 20
Miles M.3A Falcon

All those who're lucky enough to fly vintage aircraft know that - just occasionally - magic moments of total timelessness occur. I experienced such an event quite recently, while flying Peter Holloway's beautiful Miles Falcon. Cruising south from Grafham Water on a gorgeous late summer afternoon, I spotted the unmistakable shapes of the giant airship hangars at Cardington looming in the forward-swept windscreen. With the Falcon's shapely nose pointing straight at these famous structures it was easy to imagine that I was a

1936 air-taxi pilot, flying into Old Warden to pick up some chums of Richard Shuttleworth. The Falcon was designed at a time when even large international airports had grass runways, and consequently the main wheels and tailwheel are quite large. It also sports the most fabulous pair of trousers; indeed, they could almost be called pantaloons! They really are superb.
The unusual forward-swept windscreen next caught my eye. Peter laughingly revealed that the Falcon is the only aircraft he's flown where you can be dazzled when the sun's *behind* you due to reflections from this strange arrangement.
The engine is a de Havilland Gipsy Major 10 Mk2 air-cooled inverted in-line four, which produces 145hp at 2,450rpm. This is 15 horses more than standard, as the original Gipsy Major was only good for 130hp. It turns a de Havilland metal two-blade fixed-pitch and is fed from a tank in each wing. It's quite an idiosyncratic cockpit, with a reasonably modern instrument panel, and distinctly odd controls. Indeed, the plethora of levers sprouting from all around the cockpit is initially quite confusing. However, once I'd remembered where was the hand pump for the hydraulics, which was the trimmer, why the flap selector was where it was and which one worked the brakes it all started to make a bit more sense. I also made a mental note of the

throttle's close proximity to the hydraulic hand pump.

It is not the best - or worst - vintage taildragger I've ever flown. The field of view over the nose is good, but even while moving quite slowly it seemed to me that the undercarriage was not very well damped. Furthermore, as the tailwheel only castors you are rather dependent on getting the notoriously finicky 'fly-off' brakes set right. And of course, as they're operated by cables in a wooden airframe they're never the same. Why the British stuck with such a 'Mickey Mouse' system for so long remains one of aviation's great mysteries! Although I'd been feeling a little nervous (after all, it is extremely rare) as soon as the prop dissolved into a shimmering silver blur the eager ruffling of the prop wash blew away my apprehension and I settled down to work – and also enjoy myself! After all, it was a truly lovely late English summer's day – and I was flying a beautiful 1930s monoplane from a famous grass airfield.

I took off from Old Warden's runway 03 into just a hint of a Zephyr, with ambient conditions of ISA +3°C and about 200kg below MAUW, with a well forward CG. The acceleration was quite good with just a slight tendency to swing, although the ride quality was distinctly bumpy until the wing took the weight. Climbing away from Old Warden at

65kt I was pleasantly surprised to note that the VSI was showing well over 750fpm, so having reached 2,000ft in just under three minutes throttled back and set off towards Grafham Water. The thermals were already beginning to pop, and I planned to use the still air above the large lake for the stability tests. Cruising due north with the sun in my six I could clearly see what Peter meant about the windscreen. With the sun behind that odd windscreen, all those dials and the big P1 compass you certainly get some odd effects. One facet of the Falcon that is certainly worth mentioning is the super-smooth engine – it is possibly the silkiest piston I've ever flown behind. Of course, we all know that a wooden airframe does absorb vibration better than metal, but I think there's a bit more to it than that, and that this particular Gipsy Major is extremely well balanced.

By now I was really beginning to enjoy myself. It really was a stunning day to be flying, and a super aircraft to be flying in. Although chugging along at low level with that wonderful old engine rumbling away at 1,900rpm was really quite evocative, I determined not to let all my romantic preconceptions of this classic aircraft cloud my judgement and began to evaluate the aircraft qualitatively. My first impression was that the field of view was surprisingly good, bearing in mind that this machine was designed in the 1930s. Indeed, I've flown several modern aircraft whose designers would do well to take a leaf out of Miles's book. Nearing Grafham Water I commenced my evaluation of the general handling with a couple of great, sweeping turns combined with some sharp reversals. This soon revealed that the controls are quite nicely balanced, with low breakout forces and very little 'stiction' in the control circuits. Control harmony was an ideal '1-3-5', with the ailerons the lightest of the primary controls and the rudder the heaviest. Overall, it definitely didn't feel like a 76-year-old aircraft, which in my experience can sometime have remarkably inharmonious controls. The next surprise was that the Falcon is nimbler than I'd expected. Of course, it's not exactly agile, and with only me on board it was well below MAUW, yet the handling (particularly in roll) was certainly crisper than I'd anticipated. Of equal interest was an assessment of its stick-free stability. This was quite tricky. The air was getting rather unstable, while the very forward CG meant that the pitch trim lever was on the backstop. Longitudinally the stability was quite strong – the Falcon returned to the trimmed speed of 90kt after a 20kt displacement within barely two oscillations. Laterally it is weakly neutral while directionally I deemed it just barely positive, probably because the fin is not very big.

An exploration of the stall characteristics revealed that with the flaps up and the power at 'idle', a steady deceleration of one knot per second totally failed to produce a definite stall. Instead, as the ASI dropped past 60kt the buffet slowly increased until it became quite heavy. The wing eventually can't hold the weight at around 55, although it never really stops flying but just sinks straight ahead. I continued to hold the stick on the backstop and the nose gently hunted in pitch. With the flaps pumped fully down there's noticeably less buffet before the wing quits at about 40kt. With full flap it does tend to drop the starboard wing at the stall, but overall, I'd say it's fairly benign.

Cruising back towards Old Warden I set the power at Peter's recommended setting of 2,200rpm. This gave a TAS of 111kt at 3,000ft, and at this rpm the engine almost seemed like a turbine, it was so smooth. Finally, the big leather chair and its padded armrests make the Falcon a very comfortable machine to fly, and I don't doubt I could easily spend several hours in it without feeling especially fatigued.

The previous hour had flown by - both literally and figuratively -, but now it was time to start concentrating. Up in the sky it's essentially just another aeroplane, albeit a very nice one. However, vintage machines are at their most idiosyncratic in the circuit, and the Falcon is no exception. First you must set the fly-off brakes to where you guesstimate you'll get some differential braking, and then set the flap selector to down and ease the throttle back while maintaining altitude. Then, once the ASI has dipped below 70 check your hand is on the hydraulic pump's lever and not the adjacent throttle, otherwise you'll 'blip' the engine! Of course, as the flaps extend into the airflow the airspeed continues to decrease, but to open the throttle means letting go of the hydraulic pump so I lowered the nose instead and accepted the slight descent. Speed stability was good all-round the circuit, and as 03 has a slight downslope and the windsock was as limp as a wet fish I took care to nail the speed to 65, bled it back to 60 on very short final and then chopped the throttle. The touchdown was smooth, but with a tremendous 'boing' it skipped back into the air when I hit a bump. Even after the wing had clearly quit flying the Falcon still pitched and bucked around a bit during the ground roll. Touch and goes are not a good idea in the Falcon, due to the relatively high cockpit workload caused by the flap system, so I stopped, taxied back and tried again. A nice smooth and straight take off restored my confidence. This time I slowed to 70 on downwind, set the flap selector to 'down' and added a smidgen of power, then quickly pumped flaps down without losing height or gaining speed. This time I thought I'd nailed it. I left a bit more power on and it felt good and looked right all the way round, although I still got a small skip. "One more should do it" I thought as I turned downwind. Wrong! This time I smote the ground a mighty blow, and imagined I could almost hear Peter guffawing as I bounced along the runway like a kangaroo on amphetamines. Chastened, I taxied back in for a debrief. Peter revealed that the undercarriage is not stock, but from a Proctor. It really is very bouncy, and doesn't so much absorb energy as just re-direct it! It seems that the problem is that I'm not getting the stick all the way back in the flare. I like to fly with very light pressures on the controls but (as mentioned earlier) pitch trim is supplied by a spring bias system in the elevator control circuit. Consequently, the control stick forces are not linear, and the last few centimetres of travel require a fairly hefty pull on stick. I tell Peter it would've been nice to have known this before I went flying, but he just grinned and said I needed to find some things out for myself!

Chapter 21
Autumn Equinox

It's not been much of a day, but around 1600 the low-lying mist that's been hanging around like an unwanted guest that's outstayed his welcome slowly starts to shift. It's the Autumn Equinox, and as I always try and fly on days of solar significance (it must be the pagan in me) I hurry up to the strip. The little VW engine bursts eagerly into life on the third swing and by the time I've donned helmet, scarf and gloves Buzz is rocking impatiently against the chocks and the weather is improving exponentially. Mere minutes later and we're barrelling down the strip and up into the welcoming blue. The weather almost seems to be changing by the minute and cumulus cloud now dots the sky. It's turning into a beautiful evening, and as the air is unseasonably warm I decide to climb above the clouds. From a distance the cumulus look solid, but up close their diaphanous nature is apparent, and we burst through the snow-white summit of the nearest one and up into another world. It really is quite magical being above the clouds in an open cockpit; you wouldn't think that just a few millimetres of Perspex would make that much difference, but they do. Above the inversion the air is positively pellucid, providing quite exceptional visibility down-sun, and as I indulge myself by swooping and circling above the stainless white clouds, and occasionally plunging through the cloud canyons. It's truly fantastic sitting up there in the sunshine, snug and smug in the tiny cockpit. It's also surprisingly warm, but looking straight down at the ground 5,000 feet below the lengthening shadows are a powerful reminder that not only is it getting late in the year, but late in the day. Time to go home. We've bags of height, so draw the throttle right back, nudge the trim forward and start the long slide down the invisible slope that will lead us back to the strip. Now, you're going to have to allow me a little poetic licence here

Gentle Reader, but the engine (which is usually a most cacophonous device) is practically purring at this unusually low rpm. The motor matches my mood, and I decide to not adjust the throttle until after I've landed, and simply 'eyeball' my approach, from almost a mile high to touchdown. It's all good practice. Dropping steadily earthwards it occurs to me that this golden evening is made more special as from now on the days will be shorter than nights (and then the clocks go back – but don't get me started on that!) Far below I spot a large skein of geese, neatly aligned in a classic V formation and wonder, as I always do, how do they decide who flies lead? Do they take it in turns or is the leader always the one who's best at nav? And what do they use for call-signs? They can't all be called 'Goose'! Sinking slowly through the warm air with the motor quietly muttering I ruminate briefly on wonderful it is to be suspended in the sky in a home-made contraption of wood and fabric, powered by a car engine that was designed in the 1930s. I'd recently described Buzz to someone at a party, who was mortified that I'd take to the air in such a contrivance and had gasped breathlessly "That sounds awfully risky!" And I guess that in some ways it probably is — but only to me. Of course, it is self-evident that there is a need to protect third parties from unnecessary risk, but the very necessary counterpoint to that observation was probably best expounded in 1859 by the English philosopher John Stuart Mill in his essay 'On Liberty'. Mill wrote that "individuals do not need protecting from themselves", adding "'the only purpose for which power can be rightfully exercised over any member of a civilised community, against his will, is to prevent harm to others. His own good, either physical or moral, is not a sufficient warrant. Over himself, over his mind and body, the individual is sovereign.' Fine words, so why is the 'nanny state' getting ever more invasive, and why does aviation in particular seem to attract people who thrive on rules and regulations, but ignore the application of common sense? For example, is it really necessary to wear a bright yellow vest to walk across the apron of a sleepy provincial airfield in broad daylight? Not only is it illogical, it's actually counter- productive. I remember once taxiing in and as practically everyone was in a Day-Glo top it wasn't apparent who the marshaller was! Is it a cultural thing? I'm sure we'd all be more than a little surprised to learn that ISIS has a Health & Safety Executive, but are we so 'risk-averse' here in the West that even safe things are now perceived as dangerous? This may well be the case, for ironically it was an Eastern politician, Jawaharlal Nehru, who once observed that "the policy of being too cautious is the greatest risk of all" — and this is a sentiment with which I completely agree. The bottom line is that if you're too cautious you simply won't get out of bed in the morning. And that, my friend, is a very poor choice, if for no other reason than (statistically) beds are very dangerous places, as they are where most people die!

Chapter 22
Schleicher ASK-14

As the prop slows to a stop one of the great attractions of flying motor gliders manifests itself. The transition from powered to gliding flight is almost as shocking as it is sensuous. The contrast is just so vivid, but before I can really revel in the near silence of soaring flight there are some cockpit chores to take care of. A brief stab of the starter button swings the prop horizontal, swap hands on the stick then a deft pull and twist of the T-handle sprouting from the starboard side of the panel feathers the prop. Swap hands again and set the throttle and choke ready to start. Tweak the trim and settle swiftly into the core of the thermal. As the variometer needle swings confidently up towards six and the altimeter's 'hundreds' pointer starts rotating like a second hand I settle back in my seat with a smug smile. I really like soaring. I like the cerebral challenge of defying gravity by using my intellect as the engine and the atmosphere as the fuel, and the ASK-14 is well-suited to soaring flight. It's a simple machine, and the cockpit is completely in character with the rest of the aircraft, being very basic and uncluttered, and all the (very few) controls are easy to see and reach.

Although it's only got 25hp, its light, and as the prop is pitched for the climb the acceleration is acceptable. On takeoff the ailerons come alive quite quickly, enabling me to keep the aircraft balanced on the mainwheel with the tailwheel on the ground, while the delightfully low wing loading means that it waffles into the sky at about 45kt. Just press the stick forward slightly so the 14 stays in ground effect until the ASI's needle swings past 55, then gently ease up into the climb. At around 350fpm the climb rate is respectable albeit unremarkable, but improves slightly when I dab the wheel brake, release the wire safety catch that guards the undercarriage lever and then pull the lever up and back. The wheel thumps home in its well and I reduce power from a frantic 5,000rpm to a still-frenetic 4,500. The engine is still buzzing busily as I throttle back a bit more and head towards a freshly forming cumulus that already appears to have several large birds underneath it. At 1400ft I can feel the lift surging around the aircraft and almost immediately the rate of climb more than doubles. I pull the power right back, but this engine doesn't like to idle, so rather than foul the plugs a quick check that I can easily get back if it shouldn't start, then shut it down. There isn't a prop brake so I slow to almost the stall to stop the prop windmilling, motor it to the horizontal and then feather it.

The first priority is to 'secure my position' so I spend the next few minutes working the thermal up to 4,000ft. Altitude gives me time and options, while without the frantic buzz of a four-cylinder two-stroke I can begin to fully appreciate the true character of the 14. Flying it like the glider it is, is where it's at - and it's just great – for as much as I love my D.9, it's irrefutable that – at times – the boisterous bark of its unsilenced engine is quite obtrusive.

Initial impressions are that it really does feel like a K-6. The handling is feather-light and the controls crisp and precise. It doesn't seem to climb quite as well as an E (as it has slightly heavier wing loading) but has slightly better penetration (for the same reason). The field of view is exceptional. Forty knots feels very comfortable thermalling at altitude, but if ridge-running down low 50 would probably be more prudent. It quickly becomes apparent that – just like the E, when flying between sources of lift there is little to be gained using speeds in excess of 70kt as the glide angle gets very steep. It also has a small tendency to pitch up at high airspeeds and as the spring trimmer cannot compensate, the stick forces in pitch can get uncomfortably high. However, this is not as noticeable as it is in an E, possibly because it possesses marginally stronger longitudinal stability due to the more forward CG.

At the slow side of the speed envelope the stick forces are so low as to be almost unnoticeable, while the stall itself is very subtle and gentle. There is practically no pre-stall buffet, the best indications of an imminent stall being the stick position and the change in the sound of the air flow. If the speed is reduced sufficiently slowly it never really stalls, but instead simply mushes with a high sink rate.

The 14 enters a spin well and recovers promptly as soon as the correct control inputs are applied. Overall, it's a delightful aircraft to fly, although if the conditions were lively I reckon you'd tend to get bounced around a bit, just like in a K-6. On those occasions it'd require a firm hand, but on a day like today with big fat thermals it flies perfectly well without my help.

Ventilation is adequate as the canopy incorporates a large DV panel. Interestingly,

although I expected (due to sharing the cockpit with the fuel tank) that I'd smell petrol, I didn't.
I really enjoyed soaring in the 14, and could've cheerfully stayed up for several hours while having burnt probably less than a litre of fuel, but we still must shoot the air-to-air photos, so turn back towards Saltby and reluctantly decide to use the spoilers to speed my descent from 4000ft. Extending the spoilers automatically sets off the undercarriage warning horn (it has its own 9v battery and works even when the master switch is off). So, to both shut it up and expedite my descent I retract the spoilers, extend the undercarriage and then the spoilers, which work quite well. For simple spoilers they're quite powerful; they open almost 90° and are probably the best I've flown with. Having easily got back without the engine I leave it shut down. Landing with it running would be *extremely* difficult – if not almost impossible, as the combination of the high tick-over and ground effect would really prolong the float, and anyway I'm more than happy to land engine off. Back in the circuit I wait until close abeam the threshold at around 600 feet, then turn onto base and final while controlling speed with pitch and the rate of descent with the spoilers. Trim for about 50-55kt, start with about 'half spoilers' and see what happens. There's a slight nose down pitch trim change with full spoiler extension.

Landing is as undemanding as every other aspect of the aircraft. The spoilers supply adequate approach control, and I just ease them in slightly in the flare to reduce the sink rate, and sweeten the landing. It also allows me to extend the spoilers fully at touchdown, pinning the aircraft on the ground. The unsprung monowheel means a rough ride if the ground is bumpy, although the ground run is short. The stalky undercarriage ensures that if you achieve a perfect 'two-pointer' you've got a lot of alpha at touchdown, and a commensurately slow airspeed.

After a quick brief with Al and Keith who'll be in the EuroFox cameraship we launch as a flight of two and head north to Belvoir Castle, and the brief transit gives me the opportunity to examine the cruise performance. A sensible cruising speed seems to be around 65kt IAS, and as the engine uses about ten litres an hour this equates to an endurance of around two hours and a still-air range (no reserve) of about 120nm. If the cloudbase is high enough a 'saw-tooth' profile is much more efficient and would undoubtedly be the way to go.

While shooting the air-to-airs I ease the power back a fair bit and instantly sense that the engine isn't happy. It clearly doesn't like low rpm and the plugs are beginning to foul, as the motor sounds a little bit rough. A healthy handful of throttle soon clears it (followed by prompt application of spoiler to avoid sailing past the cameraship!) Like a lot of two-strokes it has quite a narrow power band and is happiest at high rpm. I shut the engine down near Saltby and move back into formation to shoot another sequence with the prop feathered, before floating down to another feather-light landing. What a delightful flying machine this thing is! It's just lovely, and I can't help but imagine how cool it would be with an electric motor and say ninety minutes of battery. It would be possible to scratch and scrape down to just a couple of hundred feet above a decent field before resorting to the electric motor, certainly much lower than I'd ever trust a petrol engine. I'm lucky in that I get to fly a lot of aeroplanes. Most of them I like, some of them I love and a few of them I want - but this one I need.

Chapter 23
Requiem for a Pawnee

"Dave, it's Keith. Bad news I'm afraid, *Gasper's* dead". "Oh no" I groaned "what happened?" Five minutes later, stunned, saddened, but not surprised, I put the phone down, poured myself a large glass of *Gentleman Jack*, drank a silent toast to an old friend and started writing. I'm not really an animist, but we all know that some aeroplanes do have character, and soul – and *Gasper* had tons of both. *Gasper*, or – as the CAA knew him, *Golf Alpha Zulu Papa Alpha*, was a Piper PA-25 Pawnee. Rugged and reliable, he was my favourite tug, and the aeroplane in which I really learned to fly. And now he was gone forever, smashed against a Welsh hillside, through sheer, crass incompetence. And that pissed me off.

Built at Piper's famous Lock Haven plant in 1970 as a 235C model, he'd had a long journey, from Pennsylvania through various agricultural operators in the US and UK, to Talgarth and the Black Mountains Gliding Club in Wales, where he was possibly the first 235hp Pawnee in the UK to be used as a glider tug. With his Hurricane-like humpbacked cockpit, long sloping nose and pugnacious, wilful appearance, to my low-houred eyes he looked a bit like a scaled-down World War Two fighter, and was the closest I'd ever got to flying such an aircraft at that time. I'll never forget the first time I climbed into the cockpit, sat on the single seat and was confronted by the imposing sight of almost four metres of aircraft between me and the spinner. Grasping the fighter-like pistol grip (complete with trigger and buttons) atop the tall control column while mentally preparing myself for my first flight – and first solo – in a Pawnee, from a tiny field halfway up the side of a Welsh mountain, I hoped he wouldn't let me down. And over the following 2,000 hours he never did. Incidentally, although aircraft typically have the feminine pronoun, to me *Gasper* was always male, because not long

after I started flying for the BMGC (and after a day of particularly strong wave rotor) I heard someone say, "that thing looks like it should have a great big pair of hairy bollocks swinging between its wheels!"
It may seem strange, but my first few years as the BMGC's resident tug pilot were some of the happiest of my life. I lived in a caravan on the airfield and was living my personal dream of flying practically every day. At 1,000ft AMSL and halfway between a mountain and a valley, on a fine morning Talgarth is probably the prettiest airfield in the UK, and a wonderful place to wake up. And if it wasn't a fine morning I didn't have to get out of bed! I had a beautiful girlfriend (who is now my wife) and lots of fun, exciting flying. I had no money, but also few possessions and no bills, so that didn't matter. What did matter was that the flying was exhilarating, and there was plenty of it. It was great! Looking back through my logbook I see we once flew on 23 consecutive days, and on one memorable day did 57 launches, peaking at an almost unbelievable 13 in 59 minutes. We also did 29 genuine field retrieves, and I could probably tell an interesting yarn about every one. Welsh fields are small! In fact, eventually the club decided field retrieves were too risky, and stopped doing them. To be fair, they could be quite fraught – but they sure were fun!

It was *Gasper* who really taught me how to fly. How to use the upslope when landing, how to cope with strong crosswinds, how to fly around mountains low-level and many other valuable lessons. I really lived – and on several occasions nearly died, in *Gasper's* cockpit. I'll never forget one week of constant easterly wave and having to fight through the vicious rotor time after time after time. It was brutal! It felt like flying in a gigantic washing machine, and at times as I struggled to maintain control I found myself wondering how much more of a beating he – and I, could take. But he never let me down.

Gasper was quite famous. He'd appeared on the BBC, ITV and S4C, and had starred in numerous articles in several magazines. Someone once sent me a page from a scale-model catalogue with a Pawnee in and yes, its registration was G-AZPA. He was one of the foundations that the BMGC was built on, being its sole tug for 35 years. Gliders and pilots came and went, but be it a bitter winter morning or a balmy summer's evening, it was always *Gasper* leading the way.

Even at the end, when he'd been cruelly betrayed by a total incompetent simply running him out of fuel and then utterly failing to manage an emergency of his own making, *Gasper* 'kept the faith' – his inherent crashworthiness saved the pilot's life. He really was a magnificent flying machine.

Well, the bottle of *Gentleman Jack* isn't as full as when I started. There's a picture propped up next to the bottle of me sleeping in a hammock next to *Gasper* while waiting for the next tow, which essentially sums the whole thing up. Although he was only one of over 5,000 Pawnees built, to me – and I suspect several other pilots, he was unique. You may think I'm getting overly maudlin about a machine, or you may not – but I'm not sure I care what you think.

Chapter 24
UCC-1 Twin Bee

As I began to add power and taxi out of our parking spot Dennis Kochan grinned at me and said, "the hardest thing about this machine is taxiing on the ground. In fact," he continued, " if you can get it to the runway you can probably fly it!" I was soon to discover how true this was! I've always been fascinated by the myriad (and often contradictory) problems posed by designing an amphibious flying machine. For example, as the machine is intended to be operated in three different mediums (air, land and water) a considerable number of variables need to be factored into the equation. These include lift and drag (both aerodynamic and hydrodynamic), and not only the centre of gravity but also the centre of buoyancy. All of the above affect the performance and handling – sometimes significantly. For example, the features that make for a seaworthy ship do not really lend themselves to the creation of an airworthy aircraft. The location of the step, design of the chines and deadrise angle of the bow, all have a profound influence on how well it will float – and fly! Excessive drag – both aerodynamic and hydrodynamic – are the 'Achilles Hull' (groan) of all flying-boats.

Both fuel-injected Lycomings started eagerly and I was soon taxiing the Twin Bee gingerly up the narrow ramp from the seaplane base to Winter Haven airport. The tailwheel castors but is not steerable, so all steering is by differential braking and power. I was amazed that there aren't any brakes on the instructor's side. The tailwheel is locked for take-off and landing. As I began the long taxi to the active runway I soon became aware that Dennis wasn't joking about it being a bit of a beast on the ground, it's quite an unwieldy machine. It was getting breezy and that big fin caught the wind, so much so that I was soon struggling to avoid 'weather cocking'. Just to complicate things further, the brakes are rather indifferent (due to being constantly immersed in water) and have a tendency to

fade. All this combined to create the hardest machine I have ever taxied. Initially, all went as well as could be expected, and I was (mostly) keeping in the middle of the taxiway.
However, just as I thought I was starting to master it, it humiliated me. I turned cautiously onto another taxiway, and across the wind. Dennis said, "watch out, it'll try to go round on you" – and it did. In a graceful pirouette the nose swung almost 90° left. I jumped on the brakes and we stopped with the nose almost at right angles to the centreline, with one wheel barely on the concrete and perilously close to a taxiway light! Judicious use of left throttle and right brake extricated me from my predicament, although almost damaging something before we'd even got to the runway definitely rattled me. I was mortified, although Dennis appeared unconcerned and waved away my embarrassed apology.
With the flaps set to 20° and all checks completed, I rolled out onto the runway, carefully lined up the Twin Bee with the centreline and let it slowly roll forward to ensure we were straight. I led with the left throttle and somewhat jerkily brought the power in, as the throttles feel very stiff. Despite being well below the 1,724kg MAUW the acceleration was quite leisurely, although at least I experienced no difficulty keeping straight as the airspeed increased. Having

picked up the tailwheel at about 30kt, I waited until the needle of the ASI reached 60, then applied gentle backpressure to the yoke and we lifted off.

As the last of the runway vanished beneath the nose, I pulled the undercarriage lever to 'up', pressed the hydraulic pump button then pulled the flap lever back and waited for the airflow to blow them up. As the flaps retracted there was a fairly significant change in pitch, which should have been easily countered by deft application of the powerful trimmer. Unfortunately, I wound it the wrong way, and was suddenly massively out of trim! Prompt winding in the other direction restored some semblance of order, but it was another blow to my self-assurance. This was not going well. I then eased the power and prop levers back to 25/25, levelled out at 1,000ft and set off for nearby Lake Marianna, for the first water landing. This went well, so as we approached the lee shore I turned the Twin Bee around, and waited for it to weathercock directly into the wind. Having completed the pre-take off checks, I pulled the yoke right back and applied full right aileron. (The engine's torque has a tendency to roll the hull in the water, and this must be countered by applying opposite aileron. Failure to do this means you drag the port float through the water, which slows acceleration). I then took a

deep breath, led with the left throttle slightly and brought the power in.
As the float came up out of the water I centralised the ailerons and began to reduce the backpressure. The nose dropped down to about four degrees as the Twin Bee surged up onto the 'step' and began to accelerate. I find water take-offs extremely exhilarating. As you accelerate across the water the hull seems to be taking a terrible pounding, and it's always very tempting to try to 'pull' the aircraft off the water. However, this is a temptation that must be resisted. The trick to taking off from water is that you must maintain the correct attitude, and not try to rotate the aircraft. If you do, you'll actually have a longer take-off run, because as the nose pitches up, everything aft of the centre of pressure pitches down, forcing more of the hull into the water. This increases drag and actually decreases the rate of acceleration. The key is to keep a constant heading with the nose at the correct attitude and the wings level. It'll fly when it's ready. That said, on rough water you do sometimes wonder just how much more of a beating it (and you) can take! A good analogy is to imagine driving really fast across the furrows of a ploughed field.
Then in one magic second the pounding stops, the wing takes the weight and you're flying! I held the Twin Bee down low so we could accelerate in 'ground affect' to the 'blue line'

speed of 70kt, before slowly easing up into the climb and raising the flaps. I then placed the nose on the horizon, drew the power and props back to 25/25 and set course for the next lake. I was very pleased with how well the take-off had gone, and Dennis was complimentary.

I now began to explore the general handling more fully. Almost straightaway I was impressed by how solid and stable the Twin Bee felt, although I didn't have time to make a thorough evaluation before we began to approach the next lake. All the primary controls are cable operated, and there is quite a lot of 'slop' in the control circuits. Although the aeroplane is reasonably responsive, the controls are quite heavy, and require large inputs. It does feel quite ponderous. I guess it is what it is – a flying houseboat! On the plus side – the visibility is great.

Dennis pointed out the next lake so I turned downwind, checked in the mirrors that the wheels were still up and had a good look at the water. Having reduced power to 18ins MP and lowered a bit of flap, I carefully retrimmed and studied the wind streaks on the surface. On base leg I drew a bit more power off and added a bit more flap, then turned onto final and extended them fully. Although a typical approach speed is 70kt, Dennis recommended 75 to give a bit of a cushion. One thing you don't want to do in a Twin Bee is get on the wrong side of the drag curve.

With the power pulled back to 12 inches I pushed the prop levers forward, then levelled off just above the lake and waited. As the keel kissed the waves I released just a hint of backpressure, then as the water took the weight drew the power off and eased the yoke back. As the Twin Bee slid backwards off the step to a foaming stop I grinned broadly, and remembered to start breathing again. "Very nice," said Dennis. I'd redeemed myself, and with my confidence returning began to enjoy the Twin Bee more and more.

The next two 'splash 'n' goes' were good, so I asked Dennis to resist the temptation to advise for the third one, unless disaster was imminent. Laughing, he agreed. Initially all went well, with a smooth take-off and accurate circuit. However, I'm so eager to impress that I tried to hold off too long. This meant we touched down with the nose slightly high, which produced a small skip and a laugh from Dennis. Annoyingly, during the take-off run I released the backpressure too early, and we porpoised slightly. Unwilling to admit defeat, I turned downwind for another go. This went well. I felt the sweet, sizzling kiss as the keel touched the waves, then the hull was soon hissing through the water.

As we planed smoothly along I drew off the last of the power, eased the yoke aft and we

fell backwards off the step in a great spume of spray. There's no doubt about it – the subtle and sublime transference of weight from wing to water is profoundly gratifying when it all comes together. Yoke back with full right aileron; I smoothly eased the throttles forward. The muted murmuring of the motors swelled to a snarl, water cascaded up and over the nose as the Twin Bee surged up onto the step and began skimming across the surface. With the throttles on the stops (full ahead both!) we gathered speed. Behind us, our wake became an ever-widening vee as our machine prepared to transform itself from a vessel to an aircraft. I could feel that the wing was taking the weight, and then we were flying again. Magic!
As we climbed away I noted that the VSI was only indicating about 500ft/min, but that's about as good as it gets. When climbing, the best technique is to simply set 25/25, then put the nose on the horizon and accept the rate this gives. It's safe to say that it doesn't have the 'Vx Factor'! Trying to climb on one engine must be a real 'seat chomping' experience!
On the way back to Winter Haven I completed my assessment of the control and stability. During the stick-free checks I had to revise my initial impression of the Twin Bee being very stable, as despite our forward CG it did feel only just stable in pitch. It was positive in yaw and neutral in roll. Slow flight revealed

benign – albeit heavy – handling, although I feel sure that you could quickly wind up with an excessive sink rate if you weren't careful. And of course, landing with excessive sink on water could end with a truly sinking feeling!
A quick look at the cruise on the way back to Winter Haven showed that at 90kt indicated, fuel flow was around 90 litres an hour. This gives the Twin Bee a range of about 270nm, plus 30 minutes' reserve.
Back at Winter Haven I pushed the undercarriage selector to 'down' and pressed the little red button to activate the hydraulic pump. After about 45 seconds I checked for the green light, and then looked in the mirrors. On final, Dennis reminded me to flare much higher than during a water landing, as the wheels hang about half a metre below the hull. Despite heeding Dennis's advice, I still touched before I meant too, but the undercarriage simply soaked it up. The taxi back across the airport and down the ramp was just as tense as it was on the way out, and I was amazed at how calm Dennis was – particularly as we trundled down the steep ramp. He really is remarkably easy-going, and an excellent instructor.
In conclusion, I absolutely loved flying the Twin Bee, despite the lack of power. Weird looking, slow, noisy and thirsty it may be – but it is amphibious! And that goes a long way in my book!

Chapter 25
Back in the Saddle

It's a beautiful September morning as I drive towards the airfield, but my state of mind it's not as it usually is on such occasions. I am edgy. It's been exactly 38 days since the accident, and the last time I flew. On that August afternoon Eskil Amdal and I may not have flown for very long but – to paraphrase Joseph Conrad – "we had been very far; sighting, verily, even the approach lights of the Great Beyond, whence no aircraft ever returns with her crew".

OK, we all like a bit of Conrad, but without being melodramatic it was quite a bad crash and we did well to survive it, thanks mainly to Eskil's superlative flying skills, and a large slice of luck. Today's agenda is to pass a

Medical Flight Test, fly a Biennial Flight Review and then go solo. Usually I'd be very much looking forward to getting airborne, and especially after a five-week layoff, but on this occasion, and for probably perfectly understandable reasons am slightly apprehensive. "The last time you went flying" nags a little voice in the back of my mind "you almost didn't come back". The prang in Sea Fury T.20 *Invincible* wasn't my first incident, but it was by far and away the worst, and there's another factor. Although I am moving quite well (bearing in mind the severity of my injuries) and quite fancy getting back in the air, I could equally leave it for another couple of weeks. However, the spectre of another coronavirus-related lockdown looms larger every day, and if that happens it could easily end up being several months until any of us can fly again, and received wisdom has always been to get back on the horse as soon as possible. I can't help but think that if I leave it too long I really might question the wisdom of going back to flying. While being grounded I read 'Thud Pilot', which is about flying F-105 Thunderchiefs over North Vietnam. The author ejected over enemy territory, was rescued, and arrived back at base a few days later, expecting to be told he was being sent home. However, he was shocked when his CO said, "You are going back to flying, aren't you" - and it was a statement, not a question. The wing had suffered substantial losses, was short of experienced pilots, and he was rostered for a combat mission the following day. He didn't have a lot of say in the matter, but I do. Do I really want to fly again? The doubts, misgivings and trepidations continue to niggle as my car rolls through the airfield gate.

One of the club's instructors, Paddy Yeoman, is also an Aviation Medical Examiner and Flight Examiner. He watches intently as I refuel and pre-flight the EuroFox, then demonstrate that I can climb in and out with a degree of alacrity and can easily reach and operate all the controls, levers and switches. Satisfied, Paddy completes the form that states I have passed the Medical Flight Test, which is promptly photographed and emailed to my AME, Dr Murray Spittal, who has been hugely supportive throughout. Dr Spittal soon replies that he has forwarded said form to the CAA and that I am now officially 'ungrounded'. Paddy then hands me over to Les Merritt who will conduct the BFR. I'm still slightly nervous as we strap in, but as soon as I press the starter button and the little engine bursts into life all my qualms and reservations are swept away by the spiralling slipstream and we taxi eagerly out to the active runway. Les is sympathetic to the fact that this is my first flight since the crash, and understands that I really wouldn't want a simulated engine failure on the very first take-off! He suggests that for the first ten minutes we simply climb up and just play amongst the clouds, and this is exactly what we do. My confidence and love of flight increase exponentially as we turn and swoop, and once Les can see that I've settled down and am back to my old self he puts me to work with a series of manoeuvres, stalls and circuits, plus plenty of practice forced landings, so I can demonstrate both to him and me that I am still safe to fly. An hour later we're back on the ground, and with a grin and one of his notoriously bad puns he signs my logbook as 'satis' and sends me solo.

A few days later and I get the chance to fly Chipmunk Mk.23 'Bumblemunk'. I like flying the EuroFox, but really like flying the Mk.23. With its single-seat, long nose, sliding canopy, powerful engine and castoring tailwheel it's a real mini-fighter, and a lot of fun. The motor is soon rumbling cheerfully to itself and I slide the canopy closed, line up, and then roar down the runway and up into the welcoming blue. It's good to be back in the sky, where I belong.

Printed in Great Britain
by Amazon

72805800R00106